W9-DFK-100

The Shaping School Culture Fieldbook

The Shaping School Culture Fieldbook

SECOND EDITION

Kent D. Peterson
Terrence E. Deal

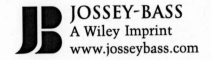
JOSSEY-BASS
A Wiley Imprint
www.josseybass.com

Copyright © 2009 by John Wiley & Sons, Inc. All rights reserved.

Published by Jossey-Bass
A Wiley Imprint
989 Market Street, San Francisco, CA 94103-1741—www.josseybass.com

No part of this publication may be reproduced, stored in a retrieval system, or transmitted in any form or by any means, electronic, mechanical, photocopying, recording, scanning, or otherwise, except as permitted under Section 107 or 108 of the 1976 United States Copyright Act, without either the prior written permission of the publisher, or authorization through payment of the appropriate per-copy fee to the Copyright Clearance Center, Inc., 222 Rosewood Drive, Danvers, MA 01923, 978-750-8400, fax 978-646-8600, or on the Web at www.copyright.com. Requests to the publisher for permission should be addressed to the Permissions Department, John Wiley & Sons, Inc., 111 River Street, Hoboken, NJ 07030, 201-748-6011, fax 201-748-6008, or online at www.wiley.com/go/permissions.

Permission is given for individual classroom teachers to reproduce the pages and illustrations for classroom use. Reproduction of these materials for an entire school system is strictly forbidden.

Limit of Liability/Disclaimer of Warranty: While the publisher and author have used their best efforts in preparing this book, they make no representations or warranties with respect to the accuracy or completeness of the contents of this book and specifically disclaim any implied warranties of merchantability or fitness for a particular purpose. No warranty may be created or extended by sales representatives or written sales materials. The advice and strategies contained herein may not be suitable for your situation. You should consult with a professional where appropriate. Neither the publisher nor author shall be liable for any loss of profit or any other commercial damages, including but not limited to special, incidental, consequential, or other damages.

Jossey-Bass books and products are available through most bookstores. To contact Jossey-Bass directly call our Customer Care Department within the U.S. at 800-956-7739, outside the U.S. at 317-572-3986, or fax 317-572-4002.

Jossey-Bass also publishes its books in a variety of electronic formats. Some content that appears in print may not be available in electronic books.

Library of Congress Cataloging-in-Publication Data

Peterson, Kent D.
    The shaping school culture fieldbook / Kent D. Peterson, Terence E. Deal. — 2nd ed.
      p. cm.
    Includes bibliographical references and index.
    ISBN 978-0-7879-9680-2 (pbk.)
      1. Educational leadership—Handbooks, manuals, etc. 2. School environment—Handbooks, manuals, etc. 3. Educational change—Handbooks, manuals, etc. I. Deal, Terrence E. II. Title.
LB2805.P39 2009
371.2—dc22

               2009012606

SECOND EDITION

PB Printing   10 9 8 7 6 5 4 3

The Jossey-Bass Education Series

CONTENTS

ACKNOWLEDGMENTS

As in our previous work together, we have had a lot of help in putting together this fieldbook. We owe a special debt of gratitude to the teachers and principals whose deep concern for students always inspires us. We thank those school leaders who shared with us stories of their schools. And for all those whose varied and creative actions have built strong and positive cultures—we applaud and congratulate you. Practitioners continue to be our best instructors in the art of culture building. And, thanks to the researchers who continue to work systematically to understand the deeper impact of school culture.

At Jossey-Bass, Lesley Iura and Christie Hakim remain the best examples of editorial guidance and support in a publishing house. Production coordinator Susan Geraghty and copyeditor Carolyn Uno provided considerable assistance that helped to refine the writing and improve the book. As usual, ongoing assistance has been invaluable. Without help from students and staff conducting tireless searches for citations and materials we would have been swamped by the many details needed for a good book. A special thanks to Erik Peterson, who created and designed many of the illustrations.

We would like to thank the many who have offered support and feedback on our writing, participated in our seminars and institutes, and provided new ways of thinking about school culture; there are too many to list all of them here. Over the years many have seen the importance of school culture and added to our understanding. Karen Kearney and Laraine Roberts of the original California School Leadership Academy; Al Bertani, Ingrid Carney, and Faye Terrell-Perkins from Chicago; and Rich Halverson from the University of Wisconsin–Madison greatly expanded our understanding of professional learning for school leaders. The many leaders and facilitators at National Staff Development Council continue to be a source of inspiration and hope that schools will become places where all children learn. We appreciate the colleagueship of Karen Dyer, Pam Robbins, Paul Bredeson, Fran Vandiver, Joan Vydra, and many others who have been excellent collaborators during our work with groups in workshops and seminars in the United States and internationally.

Our colleagues have added insights about school culture and leadership. We would especially like to thank Yi-Hwa Liou, Shelby Cosner, and Art Rainwater for thoughtful reviews of drafts and insights about cultural leaders.

At home, Ann Herrold-Peterson and Sandy Newport Deal provided their usual love and support through thick and thin, health and illness. Our kids, Erik, Russell, and Scott Peterson and Janie Deal cheered us on when we needed a little boost.

THE AUTHORS

Kent D. Peterson was the first director of the Vanderbilt Principals' Institute and is former head of the National Center for Effective Schools Research and Development. He is currently a professor in the Department of Educational Leadership and Policy Analysis at the University of Wisconsin–Madison. He lectures and consults with leadership academies across the United States and internationally. His research has examined the nature of principals' work, school reform, and the ways in which school leaders develop strong, positive school cultures. Author of numerous studies on principal leadership, he is also coauthor of *The Principal's Role in Shaping School Culture* (with Terrence E. Deal, 1990) and *The Leadership Paradox: Balancing Logic and Artistry in Schools* (with Terrence E. Deal, 1994).

Terrence E. Deal's career has encompassed several roles, including those of police officer, teacher, principal, district office administrator, and professor. He has taught at the Stanford Graduate School of Education, the Harvard Graduate School of Education, Vanderbilt's Peabody College, and the University of Southern California. He has lectured and consulted internationally with business, health care, educational, religious, and military organizations. He specializes in leadership, organizational theory and behavior, and culture. Deal is coauthor of over twenty books, including *Corporate Cultures* (with Allan A. Kennedy, 1982)—an international best-seller. His other books include *The Leadership Paradox: Balancing Logic and Artistry in Schools* (with Kent D. Peterson, 1994), *Leading with Soul: An Uncommon Journey of Spirit* (with Lee G. Bolman, 1995), and *Reframing Organizations: Artistry, Choice, and Leadership* (fourth edition, with Lee G. Bolman, 2008).

The Shaping School Culture Fieldbook

Introduction and Organization of the Fieldbook

This guide is designed to help you reflect on and hone leadership skills as you shape a better learning environment at your school where every child can learn. It may legitimate some of what you already know and are doing or add new possibilities. It also provides activities to develop cultural leadership, and it deepens and concretizes the concept of school culture by connecting it to the success of schools and students.

When gathering cases for our second edition of *Shaping School Culture,* we sought the best examples of a wide variety of cultural patterns and ways. These examples of what is possible piqued the curiosity of others. Over the past few years, interested leaders have asked us to help them learn how to read, appraise, and shape the culture of their school or district. Facing greater accountability, new curricular standards, and an expanded use of data in decision making, school leaders have often tightened structures. But the best leaders never forgot the central importance of their school's culture. Drawing on approaches we have used with thousands of principals, as well as new ideas from the leadership literature, we have distilled concrete ways to approach cultural analysis, review, and reinforcement. In this new edition, we have added more case examples, deepened the descriptions of the elements of culture, and expanded the set of strategies leaders can use to nurture positive and transform toxic cultures. We have redesigned many of the activities and added new ones to enhance the repertoire of leaders. We have written a completely new chapter on the important topic of people and relationships, the informal network in schools. This chapter describes the positive and negative roles staff take on and how to work with them. This new chapter offers strategies for making the informal network a productive element of the school's culture.

HOW TO USE THIS BOOK

This guide combines both active and reflective approaches for those who wish to invigorate their school's professional community, build trust and commitment, and return the heart and spirit to our schools. Underlying the chapters are three key processes for shaping cultural ways and traditions.

Leaders must

- Read cultural clues
- Review existing patterns and ways
- Reinforce or transform the culture

Initially, it is critical that leaders read existing cultural practices and ways to understand the key features of the culture. They need to revisit roots—the history of their district or school—and reconsider core features of the present. During this process, the leader is interpreting and intuitively identifying familiar ways that are positive as well as traditional baggage that is negative, depressing, or draining.

Second, leaders need to hold up existing customs against other possibilities. They need to identify positive, supportive norms, values, rituals, and traditions to understand the meaning of stories and to know the import of symbols. But they should also pinpoint cultural aspects that may be negative, harmful, or toxic. What positive things need more reinforcement? What time-honored but worn-out practices may need to be jettisoned?

Finally, leaders must work in a variety of ways to reinforce cultural patterns or else transform them. Even the best ways of life and meaningful rituals of a district or school need constant attention. In addition, moribund or negative features may need to be transformed, changed, or even shed. Both nurturance and change are part of cultural leadership.

THE FIELDBOOK'S ORGANIZERS: DISCUSSIONS, EXAMPLES, ACTIVITIES, AND CRUCIAL QUESTIONS

This book provides a wide variety of sources of information, inspiration, and suggestions. It can be read and used in a multitude of ways, either as a whole or in part. Each chapter begins with a discussion of the features of culture and the roles of symbolic leaders. These discussions are often followed by a set of illustrative examples.

Next, the book provides specific activities for individuals or teams that we call "Activities." Some are specifically designed as group activities, with suggestions for how to organize the session. Others are meant to stimulate reflection; in that case, the questions can become topics for dialogue or group brainstorming. These approaches have been tested and used with hundreds of educators.

Interspersed throughout the book are additional questions that we have titled "Crucial Questions," which provide the reader with ideas of interest to consider or to discuss with staff. These questions are useful for leaders to consider, but can also become the guiding topics for a staff discussion. Sometimes there are further suggestions for activities, reflections, and planning.

PART ONE

Interpreting School Culture

The Importance of Culture

Agreat deal of attention has been paid to making schools better. Policymakers want to get schools to change quickly and be more responsive to state mandates. The favored response has been to tighten up structures, standardize the curriculum, test student performance, and make schools accountable. In the short term, these solutions may pressure schools to change some practices and temporarily raise test scores. In the long term, such structural demands can never rival the power of cultural expectations, motivations, and values.

At a deeper level, all organizations, including schools, improve performance by fostering a shared system of norms, folkways, values, and traditions. These infuse an enterprise with passion, purpose, and a sense of spirit. Without a strong, positive culture, schools flounder and die. The culture of a school or district plays a central role in exemplary performance.

It is the same in any other setting. Whether it is a Starbucks coffee bar, a Southwest flight, or a Nordstrom department store, people function best when they passionately hold to a shared set of key values, central norms, and meaningful traditions.

The key to successful school performance is heart and spirit infused into relationships among people, their efforts to serve all students, and a shared sense of responsibility for learning. Without heart and spirit nourished by cultural ways, schools become learning factories devoid of soul and passion, dead cultures without spirit.

Strong, positive school cultures do not just happen. They are built over time by those who work in and attend the school and by the formal and informal leaders who encourage and reinforce values and traditions. Many schools limp along with a weak or unfocused culture due to a paucity of leadership and a lack of concern. But there are just as many other schools that are flourishing because of a strong, passionate culture. These are supported and nourished by teacher leaders and school principals who consciously or unconsciously reinforce the best that the school and its staff can become. Schools with unfocused cultures are barely surviving, whereas schools with strong, positive cultures are rich in purpose and abundant in tradition and meaning.

The central concern of this book is the development of meaningful and productive schools. Leaders must shape and nourish a culture in which every teacher can make a difference and every child can learn and in which there are passion for and commitment to designing and promoting the absolute best that is possible.

WHAT IS SCHOOL CULTURE?

The notion of school culture is far from new. In 1932, educational sociologist Willard Waller (1932) argued that every school has a culture of its own, with a set of rituals and folkways and a moral code that shapes behavior and relationships. Parents and students have always detected the special, hard-to-pinpoint esprit of schools.

Students who have attended several schools can pick up the culture immediately as they work to become part of the mix. When they enter a new school, they know that things are different in a positive or negative way that encompasses more than just rules or procedures.

Staff members who walk into a new school also pick up the culture immediately. They consciously or intuitively begin to interpret unwritten rules, unstated expectations, and underground folkways. Within the first hour of a new assignment, teachers begin to sift through the deep silt of expectations, norms, and rituals to learn what it means to become an accepted member of the school.

The culture is also embedded in an informal cultural network. Staff members often take on roles in that network. Almost every school has its collection of keepers of the values who socialize new hires, gossips who transmit information, storytellers who keep history and lore alive, and heroines or heroes who act as exemplars of core values. In contrast, in toxic cultures, one often finds "keepers of the nightmare" who perpetuate everything that has gone awry, rumor mongers who share only hostile gossip, negative storytellers who pass on pessimistic history, anti-heroines or anti-heroes who are harmful exemplars, and others who destroy positive energy and accomplishments (Deal and Peterson, 2009).

For many educators, the terms *climate* and *ethos* represent the organizational phenomena that we have described. *Climate* emphasizes the feeling and current tone of the school, the emotional content of the relationships, and the morale of the place. *Ethos* suggests shared folkways and traits, but misses the importance of ritual and ceremony.

We believe that the term *culture* encompasses the complex elements of values, traditions, language, and purpose somewhat better; therefore, we will use *culture* throughout this book. Culture exists in the deeper elements of a school: the unwritten rules and assumptions, the combination of rituals and traditions, the array of symbols and artifacts, the special language and phrasing that staff and students use, and the expectations about change and learning that saturate the school's world.

WHERE DOES CULTURE COME FROM?

Beneath the surface of everyday life in schools is an underground river of feelings, folkways, norms, and values that influence how people go about their daily work. This taken-for-granted set of expectations affects how people think, feel, and act. It shapes how they interpret the hundreds of daily interactions of their work lives and provides meaning and purpose for their interactions, activities, and work (Deal and Peterson, 2009).

Where does this aspect of schools come from? Over time, all schools develop a unique personality that is built up as people solve problems, cope with tragedies, and celebrate successes (Schein, 1985). This personality, or culture, is manifested in people's patterns of behavior, mental maps, and social norms. A simple way of thinking about culture is "the way we do things around here" (Bower, 1966).

WHY IS CULTURE IMPORTANT?

The unwritten tablet of social expectations found in a culture influences almost everything that happens. The culture influences and shapes the ways that teachers, students, and administrators think, feel, and act. For example, the following are aspects of the social expectations and values of the staff in a school:

- Whether they think improvement is important
- Whether they work collaboratively or in silos
- How much trust there is among staff members and with administrators
- Whether they feel a schoolwide responsibility for student learning
- How motivated they are to work hard
- How they feel when students do not perform well
- How they act in hallways, in lounges, and at faculty meetings
- How they dress for different occasions
- What they talk about in public or in private
- The degree of support they give to innovative colleagues
- Whom they go to for ideas or help
- How they feel about students and colleagues who are different from themselves
- Whether they believe that all students can learn
- Whether they assume that students' capacity is determined by their backgrounds
- The degree to which student learning depends solely on teaching the state-mandated curriculum.
- Whether they believe collaboration and teamwork are a good thing
- Whether they believe the state standards are potentially useful
- Whether they use data on student learning in daily planning
- Whether they see their daily work as a calling or a job

Every aspect of a school is shaped, formed, and molded by underlying symbolic elements. Although not all cultural aspects are easily shaped by leaders, over time, leadership can have a powerful influence on emerging cultural patterns. Being reflective can help leaders begin the process of reinforcing cultural patterns that are positive and transforming those that are negative or toxic.

Culture is a powerful web of rituals and traditions, norms and values that affects every corner of school life. School culture influences what people pay attention to (focus), how they identify with the school (commitment), how hard they work (motivation), and the degree to which they achieve their goals (productivity) (Deal and Peterson, 1999).

A school's culture *sharpens the focus* of daily behavior and increases attention to what is important and valued. If the underlying norms and values reinforce learning, the school will focus on that. For example, in an elementary school in the Midwest, the value was to serve the academic needs of all students. The school thus focused time, energy, and resources on curriculum and instructional strategies that helped all students become readers by the third grade. If the culture supports student learning, student learning will drive people's attention. Culture sharpens focus.

A school's culture *builds commitment to and identification with core values.* For example, in one school, staff felt they were members of a professional community, and even when they were offered higher salaries and new opportunities elsewhere, they refused to leave. If the rituals and traditions, ceremonies and celebrations build a sense of community, the staff, students, and community will identify with the school and feel committed to the purposes and relationships there. A positive culture builds commitment.

A positive school culture *amplifies motivation.* When a school recognizes accomplishments, values effort, and supports commitment, staff and students alike will feel more motivated to work hard, innovate, and support change. In one school with an unclear sense of purpose, a lack of an inspiring vision, and few celebrations of accomplishment, staff showed little energy during planning sessions. This was not the case in a Louisiana school in which staff members visited one another's classrooms regularly, shared materials and curriculum ideas, celebrated one another's new ideas and accomplishments, and even developed a regional conference on innovative teaching practices. They were motivated not because it was in their job description or contract but because they wanted to be. A positive culture amplifies motivation.

Finally, a positive school culture *improves school effectiveness and productivity.* Teachers and students are more likely to succeed in a culture that fosters hard work, commitment to valued ends, attention to problem solving, and a focus on learning for all students. In schools with negative or despondent cultures, staff have either fragmented purposes or none at all, feel no sense of commitment to the mission of the school, and have little motivation to improve. In many schools with a strong professional culture, the staff share strong norms of collegiality and improvement, value student learning over personal ease, and assume all children can learn if they—teachers and staff—find the curriculum and instructional strategies that work. In these schools, the culture reinforces collaborative problem solving, planning, and data-driven decision making. Positive, professional cultures foster productivity.

WHAT ARE THE KEY FEATURES OF CULTURE?

Culture comprises deep elements that are difficult to identify, such as norms and values, as well as more visible features, such as rituals and ceremonies. In this book, we will be closely examining all the key features of school culture.

Core Elements of Culture Addressed in This Book

- A shared sense of purpose and vision
- Norms, values, beliefs, and assumptions
- Rituals, traditions, and ceremonies
- History and stories
- People and relationships
- Architecture, artifacts, and symbols

We describe these features of culture, provide group activities for understanding them within a specific culture, illustrate them with examples from actual schools, and offer reflective questions that individuals or groups of school staff members and leaders can ponder.

CAN CULTURE BE SHAPED BY LEADERSHIP?

A key question in this book is "Can culture be shaped by leadership, or is it so amorphous and unalterable that it has a life of its own?"

Although school culture is deeply embedded in the hearts and minds of staff, students, and parents, it can be shaped by the work of leaders. As this book demonstrates, one of the key tasks of leaders is shaping culture (Schein, 1985, 2004) through myriad daily interactions, careful reflection, and conscious efforts.

The activities in this fieldbook have been used by principals and their faculties to understand existing cultural patterns and how these can be shaped or altered. Of course, this book is not a panacea. Members of a school must rely on shared values to shape culture in directions that are important, valuable, and meaningful for their school.

Vision and Values
The Bedrock of Culture

Many schools or districts have a set of values that solidly anchor daily activities with a deeper purpose. People know what is important even if they find it difficult to articulate. Deeper values and purposes shape a school's *vision*—its picture of a hoped-for future, its dream of what it can become. Such obscure and, often, veiled dreams provide a deep and rich sense of purpose and direction despite an uncertain future. This mythic side of schools is the "existential anchor" and "spiritual source" for a school's traditions, hopes, and fears (Deal and Peterson, 2009).

MISSION AND PURPOSE

At the center of a school's culture are the values that drive long-term planning, resource allocation, and daily work. Many schools have written mission statements to highlight what they are about, but their deeper purposes may be more complex and decidedly more inspirational. Core purposes hidden deep in the cultural fabric provide motivation to teachers, energize leaders to move forward, propel children to learn, and encourage parents and the community to get involved and give their support.

Trying to uncover a school's authentic mission and purpose may be more difficult than reading a mission statement. Often, it requires reading the actions and attitudes of staff and parents, probing plans and daily decisions of students, or uncovering the unstated motivations of teachers and others. In positive cultures, there is a strongly held purpose that verges on a sacred mission or an ennobling end. In contrast, in toxic cultures, purposes may be base and self-serving. Penetrating the rhetoric to find the more profound elements of a school's mission is key to understanding and shaping its culture.

How might one delve into a school's mission and purpose? Consider the basic concepts:

Values

Values are the core of what the school considers important. Values are the standards set for what is "good," what quality means, what defines excellence—in other words, what is valued (Ott, 1989). Values shape behavior, decision making, and attention, because people attend to what they consider important.

Beliefs

Beliefs are understandings about the world around us. They are "consciously held, cognitive views about truth and reality" (Ott, 1989, p. 39). In schools, staff, students, and principals hold beliefs about all the major aspects of their organization—for example, beliefs about teachers' responsibility for student learning, about students' capacities, about ethnicity and social class, about change and innovation, and particularly about the nature of students and their motivation.

Norms

Norms are the web of expectations that a group holds in regard to behavior, dress, language, and other aspects of social life. They are the unstated rules or prescriptions that staff and students are supposed to follow. In some schools, there may be norms about sharing instructional ideas, faculty meeting behavior, how to use preparation periods, or engaging in schoolwide staff development.

Assumptions

Assumptions, another key element of culture, are sometimes viewed as the preconscious "system of beliefs, perceptions, and values" that guide behavior (Ott, 1989, p. 37). Like beliefs, assumptions influence action, thought, and feelings. Members of a school may hold assumptions about the nature of teaching, curriculum, and instruction; different types of children; and leadership, among other things.

ACTIVITIES FOR UNCOVERING CULTURAL VALUES, BELIEFS, NORMS, AND ASSUMPTIONS

It is not easy to uncover aspects of a school's culture that are often hidden. However, leaders can try to identify their school's core values, beliefs, norms, and assumptions in several ways. The following activities can help leaders understand these deeper aspects.

List Six Adjectives to Describe the Culture

Gather the staff. Pass out sticky notes, and have each person list six adjectives— one per sticky note—that describe your school's culture. Display the sticky notes on a wall. As a group, start to organize the adjectives into common themes and then into positive adjectives and negative or neutral ones. This activity will give you a conceptual assessment of your school's culture. Finally, assess the meaning of each grouping. Decide which adjectives should be celebrated and reinforced and which ones should be changed. Use the following space to designate which adjectives should be celebrated and which should be changed.

_____

_____

_____

_____

_____

_____

_____

_____

_____

_____

Assess Mission and Purpose: Archeological Digs

Some ways to delve into mission are simpler than others. Conduct some archeological digs. As someone once said, "the walls have ears." What they meant was that the past and its history are embedded in the physical and emotional nooks and crannies of a building—in this case, a school building.

Examine the Change in School Vision and Mission over Time

Collect vision and mission statements from the past ten to fifteen years. You will find them in newsletters, on Web sites, and alongside school improvement plans. Make copies of them and array them in chronological order.

Then, like an archeologist, look for changes over time as well as what has continued. What are the core values of each year? Which were dropped? Do you know why? Which values and purposes have endured?

Discuss with the staff what this information tells them about the school and its deeper cultural foundation.

_____

_____

_____

_____

_____

_____

_____

_____

_____

_____

_____

_____

_____

_____

Is your school's current mission statement prominently displayed? Is it posted in the office, in classrooms, on the school's letterhead and business cards, and on coffee cups, T-shirts, and mouse pads? List all the places where the mission is displayed at your school.

_____

_____

_____

_____

_____

_____

_____

How is the mission articulated and communicated?

_____

_____

_____

_____

_____

_____

Crucial Questions

Ask yourself, "If this is our mission and sense of purpose, is it presented in various ways so that new people see what we stand for and those of the old guard are reminded of it?"

_____

_____

_____

_____

_____

Do staff, parents, and students know what the mission statement is? Are all members of the community provided with the mission in a form they can hear, know, and connect to? Is it presented in their language? Is it visually engaging to them?

Do they hear it often and in different ways—for example, through words, symbols, stories, examples, and actions?

_____

_____

_____

_____

_____

_____

Do staff, parents, and students seem excited about the mission statement? Describe how each group feels about the mission.

_____

_____

_____

_____

_____

_____

_____

_____

_____

Collect Data from Stakeholders About Their Understanding of the Culture

Ask your PTA what would help parents know and understand the mission of the school. What media are best for reaching them?

_____

_____

_____

_____

_____

Gather school mottoes and think about their meaning. Ask all the different stakeholders what they think the school really is trying to accomplish. List three major purposes mentioned by each group.

_____

_____

_____

_____

_____

_____

_____

_____

_____

_____

What people enjoy, find fun, or connect with is often what they consider important. Look for what people find joy in. Write down what different stakeholders get excited about and which stories of success they become emotional about. See how these emotionally stimulating times are part of the mission.

_____

_____

_____

_____

_____

_____

_____

Scan the Culture for Rewards and Recognition Events

Those who exemplify or advance what the school stands for and what it is working to accomplish should be recognized and rewarded. While some think that monetary rewards are the primary or, sometimes, the only reward of importance, educators, staff, parents, and students know deep down that there are other rewards. At your school, what are the rewards for accomplishing the school's mission and its goals? List them here.

_____

_____

_____

_____

_____

_____

Rewards can be *intrinsic* (for example, a personal sense of accomplishment that others support or a group's sense of achievement from implementation of successful new practices) or *extrinsic* (for example, providing money to attend a conference; telling the entire staff the story of an instructor's new teaching technique; giving out a crazy trophy to a different staff member every month who helps a student learn; sending a note to a parent volunteer who has come in to read with students; covering a class for a teacher who wants to learn from a seasoned veteran; or adding a comment on the Web site about the group of teachers who are meeting to develop writing lessons). What rewards are given during the year and for what accomplishments?

_____

_____

_____

_____

Diagram Your School's Values, Purposes, and Mission

Are there consistent patterns in the views of what is a valued mission in the school? Are there broad differences? Are there deep purposes (such as authentic learning) or narrow goals (for example, improving reading scores)? Brainstorm the core values and purposes of your school on the left side of your page. List the actions, programs, or activities that show how the school's purposes are enacted on the right.

Values and Purposes   How Enacted

_____

_____

_____

_____

_____

_____

_____

_____

_____

If you wish, draw a picture of the purposes you uncovered.

Walk the Halls and Talk to the Walls

This approach has been used successfully by dozens of school leaders to gain a deeper sense of what the school is communicating. Here's what to do:

Leave the school building during the day (and try to ignore your to-do list for a while). Walk back into the building, imagining that you are brand-new to the school, that you have never been there before.

Now, walk through the entire school. Look at what is on the walls. What do those items say to you? What do you see as you pass classrooms, art rooms, and gyms? What do you hear? Laughter, silence, yelling at kids? What kind of learning do you see going on? What do you smell and sense about the building? What is your visceral reaction?

Walk through the whole school, taking mental notes. Return to your desk and jot down what you saw, sensed, and picked up. What do these observations say about your school and its mission as actually enacted?

Does what you observed fit the written mission or something else? What should be reinforced, and what should perhaps be changed?

_____

_____

_____

_____

_____

_____

_____

_____

_____

_____

Come Up with a Song for Your Culture

Identify a song that represents the school or district's essence or a major feature of the culture. Some of the songs (or their identifying lyrics) that have been mentioned by educators include these:

"Anticipation"

"Respect"

"(I Can't Get No) Satisfaction"

"Eight Days a Week"

"9 to 5"

"Hard Day's Night"

"Wind Beneath My Wings"

"We Are Family"

"The Hero Is in You"

"The World Is a Rainbow"

"The Way We Were"

"On the Road Again"

"The Times They Are A-Changin'"

"We Are the Champions"

"Let's Get Ready to Rumble"

"The Power of the Dream"

"Bad to the Bone"

"Imagine"

"The Long and Winding Road"

"I Will Survive"

"Movin' on up a Little Higher"

"Lean on Me"

"Ball of Confusion"

"We Are the World"

"You Can't Always Get What You Want"

"Don't Fence Me In"

"Yesterday"

"Sixteen Tons"

"Whistle While You Work"

"Ain't No Stoppin' Us Now"

"Living La Vida Loca"

"If I Could Fly"

"Take This Job and Shove It"

"It's a Small World"

"Help!"

"My Way"

"Tomorrow"

"It Don't Come Easy"

List songs that represent positive aspects of your school's culture:

_____

_____

_____

_____

_____

List songs representing negative aspects of your school's culture:

_____

_____

_____

_____

_____

Divide the staff into small groups of four or five and ask them to identify two or three songs that characterize the culture. They can be songs from the earlier list or any song they know. (Often, newer staff will quickly access Apple's iTunes library for examples.) Ask the groups to share why they picked the songs that they did—that is, what messages do the songs send?

_____

_____

_____

_____

_____

_____

_____

_____

_____

_____

_____

_____

_____

_____

_____

Next, identify positive and negative aspects of the culture that are represented by the song selections. Decide which aspects to reinforce and which to work on changing.

_____

_____

_____

_____

If staff members come up with mostly negative songs, ask them what song they would like to represent the culture in three years if they could re-invigorate the school.

Using Songs with Students to Reinforce Values

Some schools have picked eight or nine songs (one for each month of the school year) that they believe represent their core values. They have used the lyrics of the songs to reinforce character education in the school by printing the words and discussing the meaning of them—one per month. Later, they have asked students to add stanzas to an existing song that expand the message.

Write an Advertisement for Your School

In preparation for this activity, you might want to cut out examples of advertisements for charter schools and independent schools. Such ads can be found in

The New York Times and most major newspapers. A search of the Internet will produce longer descriptions that schools use to engage parents and attract new students. Posting examples such as these around the room will help groups see how ads are written. Divide the staff randomly into groups of four or five, and have each group write an advertisement for your school. Ask them to imagine that they are responsible for developing an ad to be published in the local newspaper or its Sunday magazine. In as many words as they want to use, they must try to capture the school's spirit, purposes, and accomplishments. They should include pictures, symbols, photos, quotations, or a combination of these that would attract new students, teachers, or parents. Use this space for your advertisement.

Put the advertisements prepared by the groups on chart paper, and post them on the walls. Have each group pick a spokesperson to present its ad. Or have the groups film an ad.

As you listen to the ads, make notes on which major themes are repeated and what values are reinforced.

_____

_____

_____

_____

_____

_____

_____

_____

_____

_____

_____

_____

Putting School Advertisements in the Media

Your next step might be put to use the themes you have observed in the ads in a digital advertisement with a maximum length of sixty seconds. Draft or story-board your ad in the space on page 30. Use whatever symbols or local actors—students, teachers, volunteers, or others in the school community—that people feel best represent the school. Show the ad on local access television, or put it on your school's or district's Web site, in your school's electronic newsletter, or in a local online paper.

Design a Symbolic Representation—A Heraldry Shield

In medieval times, kings and queens had court artists design a heraldry shield that included symbols of their values, their accomplishments, and their honor or might.

Design a heraldry shield that depicts your school's core values and purposes.

To get started, divide the shield into parts. For example, it might be helpful to divide the shield into four quadrants and have each quadrant represent some aspect of your school's culture and values. You can pick what to put in each quadrant. Here are some ideas: three or four key values; core programs or instructional themes of the school (for example, performing arts, math and science, public services, or entertainment technologies); instructional approaches that are central to the school's mission; mascots, mottoes, or logos; what a graduate will look like; or major accomplishments from the past five years. Draw the shield in the outline that follows.

Have your staff members design their own shields, as individuals or in small groups. Discuss the symbols and the meaning in what people have created. Discuss all the different values and skills represented.

Have Students Make Heraldry Shields

Ask students to develop their own heraldry shields to represent their school or classroom. See how they view the core values and mission of the school or classroom, and write your observations here.

_____

_____

_____

_____

_____

_____

_____

_____

_____

_____

Pick one of the shields (or combine the best of several) and place it in a prominent place in the school or put it on the school's Web site as another representation of the mission of the school.

Encourage Metaphorical Thinking

It is useful to encourage creative approaches to understanding deeper interpretations and understandings. Metaphorical thinking provides an engaging way to read a school's culture. Here's an approach that has worked with school leaders around the country:

_____ ✳ _____

Gather the staff, students, or parents of your school community, and ask everyone to write a metaphor for the school (adapted from Gordon, 1961). Distribute sticky notes (three by five inches or larger) to everyone, and ask them to complete this metaphor:

If my school were an animal, it would be a _____,

because_____

_____

Emphasize the importance of giving reasons for the choice. Staff members sometimes select the same animal, but for different reasons. For example, one staff member said the school was like an octopus "because it had arms reaching in every direction and no backbone." Another staff member also picked an octopus, but "because it has strong arms reaching out for nutrients and connected in the center."

Take all the metaphors and put them on a wall (or if there is some conflict among the staff, type them up and print them out so that everyone remains anonymous). Divide the staff into small groups, and have them discuss the metaphors, looking for underlying meanings, themes, and patterns that they see in them. For example, at one school, many of the metaphors were about female predators (lionesses, bears, cheetahs). Many had a common theme of care and nurturing the young but hostility toward other adults who might come close. The discussion turned toward how staff members could become more respectful and supportive of each other. In another school, a number of metaphors identified animals that changed during their life cycle (chameleons, butterflies, tadpoles). The staff felt proud of its ability to cope with changes in their school.

Have the groups write the themes on chart paper (positive themes on the left, negative themes on the right). Have the whole staff discuss what these themes say about the school and which themes they want to keep or discard. List those to keep and those to discard below:

_____

_____

_____

_____

_____

_____

_____

_____

Other Uses for Metaphors

This exercise can be used to gain a sense of a group's feelings and attitudes about specific situations. At the end of the year, ask everyone individually to write a metaphor for the past nine months. Ask, "If the year were an animal, which one would it be, and why?" One can use this exercise to get a sense of a school's culture in general, the past year, a new program, or any significant event in the life of a school. List below when you might use this technique to understand staff feelings and attitudes.

_____

_____

_____

_____

_____

_____

_____

_____

_____

_____

_____

Draw a Picture of Your School's Culture

A good initial exercise that will help you read the culture is to have staff draw pictures representing the school's culture. Have each person draw a representative depiction of the school's culture on a sheet of eight-and-a-half-by-eleven-inch paper, using pictures, words, symbols, and color. Encourage creativity and respect for those whose art skills are limited. Draw your picture here:

Try not to make suggestions about what the pictures should look like. This activity has been used with dozens of groups, including districts, schools, departments, and staff working with kids at a specific grade level. The range of diagrams and drawings have been incredible—from simple organizational charts with no connecting lines to beehives and anthills, from apple trees with some branches bearing fruit and others withering and dying to solid oak trees with deep roots (a strong foundation) and new little oaks starting from the acorns dropped by the parent tree. The range of possibilities is wide; let the creative juices flow.

Have the staff members move into small groups to share their pictures and what they mean. Look for implicit themes such as collaboration, support, nurturant relationships, or negative or hostile elements. Based on the pictures, discuss the overall view of the school as a whole group.

Identify the Heroines and Heroes of Your School

Every school has a set of exemplars, symbols of what is best about the people who work at the school. These are the school's heroines and heroes. These members of the cultural network represent role models for the culture. While heroines and heroes are discussed in more detail in Chapter Six, take some time now to consider what values and beliefs about being an educator are embedded in their stories.

Use the following space to identify the core values and purposeful actions of the heroines and heroes of your school's culture. Consider what they have accomplished and what their stories communicate. (Find time to recognize and celebrate what they represent to the school, for they are living mission statements.)

Crucial Questions
Who are your school's heroines and heroes? What are their stories?

_____

_____

_____

_____

_____

_____

_____

_____

_____

_____

_____

_____

_____

_____

Can you brainstorm a list of their accomplishments and what they mean?

_____

_____

_____

_____

_____

_____

_____

_____

What values are communicated by the actions of your school's heroines and heroes? (For example, dedication, perseverance, belief in students, a focus on learning and personal development of children, innovation, energy, commitment, or other values)

_____

_____

_____

_____

_____

_____

How do their actions represent or symbolize the sense of purpose and mission of your school?

_____

_____

_____

_____

_____

_____

_____

_____

Can you list ways to recognize and celebrate the exemplary work of your schools' heroines and heroes? Think of simple and more complex approaches to the recognition of accomplishments.

_____

_____

_____

_____

_____

_____

_____

_____

FINAL THOUGHTS

Examining values and beliefs, mission statements and mottoes helps you look deeply at your school's culture. Ask your staff, "Which of these values and purposes should we keep? Which do we choose to discard?"

Ritual and Ceremony
Culture in Action

A life devoid of ritual and ceremony would be one without richness and zest. The small daily rituals of our lives provide time for reflection, connection, and meaningful experience. Imagine a day without morning coffee or a glance at the newspaper, without the late afternoon break with colleagues, absent the nightly walk with a loved one, or checking for an e-mail from a son or daughter in college. Rituals help keep us connected, foster renewal, and provide opportunities to bond with others we work or live with.

Rituals and ceremonies often occur in regular patterns over the course of a year, punctuating the flow of months and providing bookends for cyclical endeavors. Much richness and connection would be lost if we had no opening school ceremony, homecoming, Halloween, Thanksgiving, Hanukkah, Christmas, Kwanzaa, New Year's Eve, Passover, Easter, or Cinco de Mayo.

Without ceremonies and traditions to mark the passage of time, honor the accomplishment of valued goals, or celebrate the possibilities of new hopes and dreams, our lives would stagnate, dry up, and become empty of meaning and purpose. These episodic cultural events help keep us all connected to the deeper values of our labor and of the institution to which we have committed our lives. Without ceremonies, traditions, and rituals, we could easily lose our way amid the complexity of everyday life at work.

Rituals and ceremonies help make the intangible graspable and the complex understandable. They allow us to act out meaning and values that would otherwise be difficult to understand and feel. Communal events help bond us together and build trust.

Social events are the outward expression of the deeper possibilities of culture and its core values. They are to school culture what the movie is to the script, what the concert is to the score, and what the sculpture is to the values of the artist (Deal and Kennedy, 1982). They reinforce and continue cultural values and beliefs.

Education—that is, seeing that children learn in a safe and supportive environment—remains one of the most complex and challenging of all social endeavors. In many ways, building cars, designing ships, and developing software are simple in comparison. Ritual and ceremony are probably more important in schools than in businesses because the product and the services are so complex and the important outcomes hard to measure. Communal gatherings are especially important in education as ways of maintaining the energy and focus of hardworking staff. Symbolic social events help staff members through the daily routines and demands of teaching and foster professional community and a spirit of caring and camaraderie. Rituals and gatherings bind the many groups of a school into a whole and provide times to decompress and have fun. For all of these reasons, leaders need to bring ritual and ceremony into the lives of teachers and students, noncertified staff and volunteers, parents and community members.

In this era of intense scrutiny and high-stakes accountability, schools need to rejuvenate rituals and energize key traditions to keep spirit and soul alive. Learning for both students and teachers is enhanced through meaningful traditions, frequent rituals, community ceremonies, and regular celebrations that nurture and nourish cohesion, motivation, and focus.

RITUALS

Rituals are processes or daily routines that are infused with deep meaning. They are more than just technical actions. Rituals help transform common experience into uncommon events. Every school has hundreds of routines, from taking attendance in the morning to exiting procedures in the afternoon. When these routine events can be connected to a school's mission and values, they summon spirit and reinforce cultural ties; for example,

- Some schools provide students with welcome kits that are filled with school supplies, books, and a DVD about the school. Other schools assign each student a buddy or mentor.

- At Ganado Primary School in Ganado, Arizona, visitors are taken on a tour by an articulate Navajo tour guide who shows them through the hallways and into the central instructional media center (IMC), which features a display of superb Navajo rugs from local weavers.

- In a school in the Midwest, new teachers have a mentor who tells them the history of the school, takes them on a tour of the community, explains the informal rules, and provides a $50 card for a supply store.

- In another school, new staff members are given a school coffee cup and provided with a list of all the accomplishments and awards that the school and its teachers have received as a way of connecting them with the culture of the school. In addition, the school's mission is explained and pictures of graduates are shared.

TRADITIONS

Traditions are significant events that have a special history and meaning and occur year in and year out. Unlike ceremonies, they need not be large communal events. Traditions are part of the history of the school and tie people to its cultural roots. There are many traditions in schools. Here are some examples:

- Meeting in the summer for a barbecue and games

- Holding regular faculty retreats to plan school improvement efforts

- Arranging school overnights or camping trips for students

- Painting the boulder in the front of the school as a senior event

- Holding a school art auction to garner support from parents and the community

- Serving certain foods (local barbecue or fruit pies) during ceremonies

- Having the school storyteller and historian at retirement parties

- Framing mementos of staff and student accomplishments and recognitions and hanging them in the halls

- Celebrating the school's benefactors in a yearly ceremony

- Wearing academic robes at graduation

- Holding a gallery night every spring to show the best art of the year

- Recognizing nonathletic successes in a pep rally
- Making food for fellow staff members when there has been an illness or tragedy in their family

When people have traditions that they value and appreciate and that occur regularly throughout the year, they have a foundation for weathering challenges, difficulties, and change. Following are more examples of traditions:

- In one Midwest school, every adult who works in the school goes to the kitchen and shares cinnamon toast in the morning.
- In another school, teachers traditionally share workshop reports, evaluations, and stories after returning from professional development opportunities.
- In one school, the staff starts the faculty meeting by telling stories—sometimes funny, sometimes serious—about students in their classes.
- At Coral Springs Middle School in Florida, when Fran Vandiver was principal, faculty meetings would start with a story. Vandiver would tell a story of a teacher or staff member who had done something special to help a student or parent and then present that person with a school coffee cup.

CEREMONIES

Ceremonies are elaborate, culturally sanctioned events that provide a welcome spiritual boost. Most schools have formal ceremonies that mark transitions in the school year. These periodic communal events bind people to each other and shape unwritten cultural values.

Ceremonies are times to come together to connect to deeper values and purposes. Through ceremonies, a school celebrates successes, communicates its values, and recognizes the special contributions of staff, parents, and students. Each season of the year can provide time to communicate ceremonially through communal events, the symbolic glue that binds a school together.

- Opening-day ceremonies greet new members.
- Fall holiday ceremonies mark the transition into winter.
- Second-semester ceremonies mark the beginning of a new learning time.
- Ceremonies before state tests can forge a commitment to do well.

- Retirement ceremonies mark the end of a career and note the contributions that people have made to the school.

- Graduation ceremonies mark the success of teachers and students to complete a course of study and the transition to the next life stage.

- End-of-the-year ceremonies provide closure for the year's efforts and a take-off point for the coming year's goals.

Celebrations are a type of ceremony that combines rituals, symbols, and stories into a positive festival of energetic fun, humor, and acknowledgment of successes. Often less serious and higher in energy than other ceremonies, celebrations often include music, cheering, and wit.

- At every faculty meeting in one middle school, the staff celebrated a teacher who had developed a new idea, instructional approach, or curricular innovation. The teacher was given an enlarged representation of Munch's painting *The Scream* to keep in the classroom.

- In a Utah high school, one or two pieces of student art are purchased every year, a short speech is given in a small event, and then the art is added to the school's collection, which honors a student who died before she could go on to an art career in college.

- A small southern district celebrated the classes that had improved the most on various measures of achievement with an ice cream social in the spring.

- In many schools, staff celebrate the completion of a master's degree or a doctorate with banners and cheers.

- Superintendent Terry Grier organized celebrations for high school students who had taken numerous Advanced Placement (AP) classes and then passed the AP exams by giving all of them a chance to win a new car donated by a local dealer.

- Many schools have mini-celebrations when, for example, their athletic team moves on to the state tournament, their forensic team wins a regional competition, or a student becomes a state scholar.

Celebrations are opportunities to recognize the accomplishments of individuals or groups. They demonstrate possibilities for success and build a sense of pride in a school.

ACTIVITIES FOR ASSESSING AND IMPROVING RITUALS, TRADITIONS, AND CEREMONIES

Assess School Rituals

Schools have many types of rituals. You can understand and shape your school's culture by reflecting on common rituals. Ask yourself what your school's rituals are and what they communicate. This section considers several types of rituals. Determine which of these are performed in your school, and reflect on their meaning.

Greeting Rituals

Every organization specifies ways to greet new people. These rituals communicate how a school values various groups. How parents or new staff members are welcomed is particularly important.

Crucial Questions

How are new teachers acknowledged in faculty meetings? How are they introduced? Does their supervisor provide a rich and personal description of who they are and what they have accomplished or simply list their name and position?

_____

_____

_____

_____

_____

_____

How are new students and their parents or caregivers greeted? Are they greeted in their primary language? What are they told about the school? What are they given to help them connect and adjust? Are books, materials, and school supplies offered to those who have just moved into the neighborhood?

_____

_____

_____

_____

_____

_____

_____

_____

_____

_____

Unfortunately, those who arrive at times other than the beginning of the year are often given short shrift. New staff, students, and parents who come in the middle of the year should be greeted with the same energy and attention as are given to those who arrive at the beginning of the year.

_____ ✳ _____

What are the welcoming rituals for midyear transfers?

_____

_____

_____

_____

Transition Rituals

Transition rituals provide staff members with a way to move from one role, program, or approach to another or to end an era symbolically. Change always brings with it some sense of worry or concern. Without transition rituals, the sense of loss can increase and cause problems.

Crucial Questions

Does your school have significant rituals for the following major transitions during the year? What are these transition rituals like? Do they help the staff through the changes?

When school begins:

_____

_____

_____

_____

After winter break:

_____

_____

_____

_____

Before major state tests:

_____

_____

_____

_____

_____

At the end of the year:

_____

_____

_____

_____

_____

If you do not have one or more of these rituals, suggest some.

_____

_____

_____

_____

_____

Career transitions are important too. What are the rituals when staff members receive tenure, work for five or ten years at the school, or retire?

_____

_____

_____

_____

_____

_____

_____

_____

Some schools have complex retirement ceremonies that include stories, old photos, artifacts from decades of teaching, and symbolic gifts (one school provides pins designed by students; another, a print of the school; another, a paperweight that displays the school's mission).

Testing Preparation Rituals

Most schools are facing increased testing and accountability. Schools have always held pep rallies before athletic contests, and now many are holding rallies before testing periods. School rituals that recognize challenges ahead can motivate effort and ease tensions.

Crucial Questions

What special rituals take place before testing periods—for example, a school pep rally, a free breakfast, or new pencils? Is there a special edition of the school newsletter? Pins to encourage effort?

_____

_____

_____

_____

_____

_____

Does your school recognize success after test scores come back? If so, describe how. If not, suggest how it might do so.

_____

_____

_____

_____

_____

_____

Initiation Rituals

All cultures have rituals for newcomers. Whether one is aware of it or not, new people are initiated into a school through words and deeds. How people are initiated influences their understanding of the school's values and their commitment to the organization.

Crucial Questions

Are new staff members initiated into the school through formal mentoring or informal induction? What are some of the ways in which this is done?

_____

_____

_____

_____

_____

_____

How are the norms and values, vision and dreams of your school communicated? Do new staff members get copies of the mission statement, hear stories of success, or learn the history of the school?

_____

_____

_____

_____

_____

_____

Are the yearly rituals and ceremonies at your school described and discussed, or do they simply happen? How is the importance of these events communicated? Are new staff given roles in these ceremonies?

_____

_____

_____

_____

_____

_____

Are there formal initiation rites or introduction rituals to connect new staff members with the existing culture? For example, one school requires multimedia introductions and another has a heraldry shield designed for each new staff member. Write down some of the initiatory or introductory rituals of your school here.

_____

_____

_____

_____

_____

_____

How could you improve the greeting and introduction of new staff members?

_____

_____

_____

_____

_____

_____

_____

Closing and Ending Rituals

The closing of a school and the ending of a program are key times to hold rituals. These are always difficult times and need to be recognized symbolically and socially. Without rituals, needed psychological closure may not occur.

Problems can develop if there is no closure or ceremonial gathering. In one school, a longtime staff member left and said she wanted no good-byes. One day, her desk was empty, her walls bare of the photos she had taken of students, and her bookshelves empty except for a broken coffee cup. The staff continued to mourn for the lost staff member into the next year, draining its emotional energy for months.

Losses of beloved mission statements can be felt deeply as well. In a Florida district, staff had worked hard to develop a well-crafted mission statement and set of beliefs about education that truly captured their hopes and dreams. The mission statement was professionally printed in a small folded pamphlet that fit neatly into a wallet, so staff literally carried the mission with them every day. They valued it. Then, a new superintendent wanted to bring in a new direction and demanded that all the old mission pamphlets be turned in to the office. Many were. But most staff members secretly kept theirs clandestinely in their possession, holding on to a commitment to what they believed. When meeting, teachers would pull out their old, worn pamphlets and remember what they valued. They held on, in part, because there had been no transition ceremony or respect for the past.

Crucial Questions

Recall the last time a program ended, a staff member left, a unit closed, or a textbook was retired at your school. How was the event affirmed? Was an artifact or remembrance of the person or program kept as a historical marker of it?

_____

_____

_____

_____

_____

What rituals have most helped people through endings at your school? Did people tell stories about the departed staff member or program? Was there laughter, nodding heads, or perhaps some crying? Why did the rituals work well?

_____

_____

_____

_____

_____

_____

_____

Consider these ways to get closure:

- Respect the feelings of loss or sadness that accompany change
- Carefully move out the old materials, uniforms, or artifacts; perhaps even archive them
- Share stories about the program that is ending or the people who are leaving, and keep written records or audio or digital recordings of these stories

Have there been endings at your school that have not had proper closure? A ritual may be needed to promote healing and letting go. What kind of ritual would you design to help your school community gain some closure on a past event or the departure of a person?

_____

_____

_____

_____

_____

_____

_____

Identify and Interpret Your Traditions

Traditions are events or actions that occur from year to year and establish a sense of continuity, reinforce values, and build community. School leaders actively assess their traditions and strive to make them more meaningful.

Crucial Questions

What are your school's traditions, and what meaning do they have for faculty, students, and the larger community?

_____

_____

_____

_____

_____

_____

_____

What messages do your school's traditions communicate? How do they reinforce your school's culture?

_____

_____

_____

_____

_____

_____

_____

_____

Identify Core Traditions and Ceremonies

Following are some ceremonies found in schools. Track the ceremonies in your school that occur during the year. Identify which of these traditions and ceremonies occur in your school and what they celebrate.

———————————————————— ✳ ————————————————————

What is your school's **opening-day ceremony** to rebind staff and build community? What are the important rituals during that day? What symbols, messages, artifacts, and stories are used to build a sense of community and connection to the mission?

_____

_____

_____

_____

_____

_____

_____

_____

What are your **seasonal ceremonies** (such as Cinco de Mayo, Black History Month, or homecoming)? How do these connect to your school's core culture and sense of mission?

Fall

_____

_____

_____

_____

_____

Winter

_____

_____

_____

_____

_____

Spring

_____

_____

_____

_____

_____

Does your school have any **management ceremonies** to help accomplish and acknowledge administrative tasks, such as school improvement ceremonies, celebrations associated with the presentation of the school's yearly goals, or parties when test results arrive?

_____

_____

_____

_____

_____

_____

What management ceremonies or rituals might your school add to its calendar?

_____

_____

_____

_____

What **integrative ceremonies** does your school hold in order to meld social, religious, and ethnic groups? When do they occur? Are all the diverse groups of your school included and noted during these ceremonies?

Fall

_____

_____

_____

_____

Winter

_____

_____

_____

_____

Spring

_____

_____

_____

_____

At your school, what **recognition ceremonies** pay tribute to the special accomplishments of individuals and groups, thereby forging pride and respect? When do they occur?

_____

_____

_____

_____

_____

What set of accomplishments is recognized with ceremonies? Does this set match the core values and goals of your school? What might you need to add?

_____

_____

_____

_____

Do you hold **homecoming ceremonies** to reconnect graduates with your school and to develop a sense of history and continuity? Homecoming events can be important in communities where students do not sense much hope for their future. Seeing real, live alumni who have succeeded can build a strong sense of hope among students.

_____

_____

_____

_____

_____

What have alumni of your school accomplished? Do you keep a recording (perhaps a DVD) of these accomplishments that is available to students and parents?

_____

_____

_____

_____

_____

Some schools hold special **ceremonies to mark the beginning or end of unique events** such as completion of a new addition to the school, reaching a specific level of academic achievement, or bringing in a new program (for example, Advanced Placement classes, an International Baccalaureate program, or becoming a theme school). What special ceremonies does your school hold?

_____

_____

_____

_____

_____

How are special events planned at your school? What message is sent? Is the event recorded for posterity?

_____

_____

_____

_____

_____

_____

All schools face loss at some point. What **memorial ceremonies** are held to remember the contributions of staff, students, or community members who are no longer at the school and recognize the school's loss of them? Sometimes memorial ceremonies become traditions that occur every year to remember a staff member or student. How have memorial ceremonies been used to reinforce core values and a sense of purpose at your school?

_____

_____

_____

_____

_____

_____

_____

Map Traditions and Ceremonies over the Year

Ceremonies are key features of a school's culture that occur at different times throughout the year. What are all the ceremonies at your school? What message, value, or norm do the ceremonies communicate and reinforce?

On the right side of the following chart, write the large and small traditions and ceremonies that your school observes over the year, constructing a time-line for a typical year. Note any periods of time that have few of these important events. Note on the left side of the chart the administrative and programmatic tasks that occur each month.

Be especially aware of any ceremonies or traditions that are weak or dead; it may be time to either drop or resuscitate them.

Map Administrative Tasks and Ceremonies Over The Year

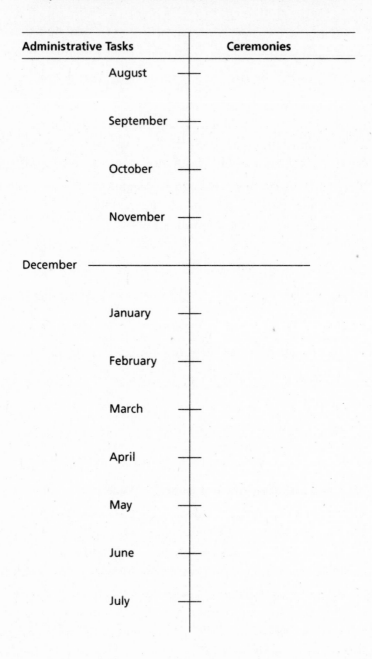

Administrative Tasks	Ceremonies
August	
September	
October	
November	
December	
January	
February	
March	
April	
May	
June	
July	

Identify the Elements and Meaning of Ceremonies

It is essential to assess the meaning and purpose of all aspects of a ceremony. In the following space, list on the left the elements of one of your key ceremonies. Next, reflect on the symbolism and meaning of that element, and detail it on the right. Finally, identify any elements that do not communicate what you would like them to and suggest ways to improve their message.

Ceremonial Element   **Symbolism, Meaning, or Value**

_____

_____

_____

_____

_____

_____

_____

_____

_____

_____

_____

_____

_____

_____

_____

Reflect on Dead or Dying Ceremonies

Not all ceremonies maintain their vibrancy and purpose over time. Some are already dead and ought to be ended, but others that are dying should be revived and resuscitated. Dead ceremonies no longer reinforce cultural values or nurture the school community. Positive, energizing ceremonies support the core values of the school and build a sense of connection and commitment among staff, students, and parents.

Are there any ceremonies in your school that no longer have meaning, are simply seen as requirements, or reinforce negativity? Some ceremonies are dead, dying, or dormant. Decide what to do to revive moribund ceremonies that you wish to keep. Let the others go.

Describe a dead ceremony that you want to revive and suggest actions to resuscitate it:

_____

_____

_____

_____

_____

_____

List a dead ceremony that needs to be ended and buried. Then suggest how to effectively release the ceremony (and the school) from its misery:

_____

_____

_____

_____

_____

_____

Design Successful School Ceremonies

Ceremonies offer the opportunity to showcase successes, reinforce effort, and cement the social relationships that are so important to making schools caring, safe, and productive. Ceremonies can celebrate the start of a school year, recognize the accomplishments of students and staff, provide closure to a long career when someone retires, and mark other important events. Following is a list of the elements one finds in ceremonies (Deal and Peterson, 2009). It can be used as a planning list of things to consider when designing or redesigning a ceremony or celebration.

Elements to Consider Including in a Ceremony

☐ A special purpose that is linked to core values of the school

What is this purpose? _____

_____

_____

☐ Symbolic clothing and adornments

Describe these: _____

_____

_____

☐ Meaningful symbols, signs, banners, flags, or artifacts

List the symbols and artifacts to include and why they are important: ____

_____

_____

☐ Stories of history, accomplishment, and unusual effort

Which stories or examples will you use? _____

_____

_____

☐ A distinctive manner of speaking or presentation

What is the tone you wish to project? _____

_____

_____

☐ An invocation of deeper purpose and values

How will you invoke these deep values? _____

_____

_____

☐ Who is invited and where they will sit

List who will participate: _____

_____

_____

☐ Recognition of those who have shown exemplary commitment

Who will be recognized at the event? _____

_____

_____

☐ Appropriate and varied music

What music will be played? Why that music? _____

_____

_____

☐ A carefully selected, attractive setting

Where will the event be held? Why there? _____

_____

_____

☐ Delicious food or drink

List what will be served: _____

_____

_____

☐ Value-filled language and commentary

What special words or language will be used? _____

_____

_____

☐ Ritual acts and ongoing traditions

How have these ceremonies traditionally been conducted at your school? What rituals or traditions need to be included in order to connect with prior events? _____

_____

_____

☐ The recounting of sagas, legends, or stories about the school

What stories or sagas need to be recounted at this event? _____

_____

_____

☐ An ending on a high point

How will you end the event so that people feel energized and excited as they leave? _____

_____

_____

Ceremonies should mirror and signal the values of your school as well as its vision for the future. Following are questions to ask as you design or redesign a ceremony. Space is provided for you to jot down ideas or notes as you think about each question.

Crucial Questions

What message will be sent by the ceremony? Is it clear and well articulated?

_____

_____

_____

_____

_____

_____

How will the school bond with its larger community through this ceremony? Are parents, community members, and retired staff included?

_____

_____

_____

_____

_____

Who will be involved in the actual event? Will various stakeholders be part of the presentations, speeches, and activities?

_____

_____

_____

_____

_____

Will the school's core values be communicated in multiple ways—for example, through stories, videos, music, and images?

_____

_____

_____

_____

_____

Will there be opportunities for the group to actively recommit to the school's mission? Will staff, students, and parents be able to sign on to the goals of the year, recommit verbally, or stand up and be counted?

_____

_____

_____

Will there be histories or stories of accomplishment and dedication told by the school's best historians or storytellers? These stories can be told in person or through a recorded presentation.

_____

_____

_____

_____

Will new members of the community be appropriately recognized? Will there be in-depth introductions with details of who they are, what they have already accomplished, and interesting personal information?

_____

_____

_____

_____

Will the costume or dress for the ceremony be appropriate and symbolic? Jeans and sweats are fine for repainting the gym, but ceremonies should be attended with some consideration of dress, whether you choose business casual, a sport coat, or tailored clothes. Your choice will send an important message.

_____

_____

_____

_____

Will symbols that communicate your school's values and expectations be displayed? Is there a mascot, flag, banner, photograph, or artifact of the history being related that should be part of the event? Be sure that appropriate symbols and artifacts are included.

_____

_____

_____

_____

_____

If awards will be presented, are they appropriate to the accomplishment and do they convey the value of the contribution?

_____

_____

_____

_____

_____

Are the location and setting of the ceremony appropriately serious or fun? Will the setting be a hot lunchroom or a local college auditorium? Will the ceremony begin in one setting and move to others that will provide time to discuss and reflect?

_____

_____

_____

_____

_____

Will there be music to reinforce the tone and feeling of the event? Is the sound quality of the music clear, appropriate, and energizing? Is it connected to past music or part of a tradition of new songs and music?

_____

_____

_____

_____

_____

_____

Will carefully selected food or drink be part of the ceremony? Will the food be special, varied, and of high quality? It need not be expensive, but it should show attention to detail.

_____

_____

_____

_____

Will elders be recognized and celebrated at the ceremony? Will senior staff, retired teachers, alumni, elderly volunteers, or dedicated community members be involved and acknowledged?

_____

_____

_____

_____

Does the sequence of events provide the right flow of ideas, actions, and values? Will there be appropriate pacing, transitions, and management of energy levels in order to build a sense of excitement, connection, or commitment? Mapping the flow of events is crucial to a powerful ceremony.

_____

_____

_____

_____

_____

_____

Will the tone of speeches, music, and stories be appropriate to the symbolic meaning of the event? What tone, mood, tenor, or ambience do you want to set? Whether you wish the event to be energizing, serious, fun, rousing, or some combination of these, it is important to reflect on the mood you want and plan what it will be.

_____

_____

_____

_____

_____

_____

What do you want participants to leave with? What feelings, ideas, and goals do you want them to take with them? How will you reiterate your themes toward the end of the ceremony? Whether the recapitulation is accomplished through words, actions, or symbols, it should be dramatic and clear.

_____

_____

_____

_____

_____

_____

Finally, have the appropriate speeches and exhortations been offered for current programs and reforms—celebrations for those that are alive and well, support and resuscitation for those needing nurturance, and funerals for those that have ended or died?

_____

_____

_____

_____

_____

_____

_____

_____

_____

_____

_____

_____

_____

_____

_____

FINAL THOUGHTS

It is absolutely crucial to have positive, regular, and meaningful rituals, traditions, ceremonies, and celebrations to nurture and sustain the culture of a school. Although ceremonies are the more serious and significant communal events of a culture, it is important to recognize, honor, and celebrate accomplishments big and small. Without these communal events, a school's culture may drift and wander, or wither and turn toxic.

History and Stories
The Importance of the Past

Every organization has a history that has shaped its people, programs, and culture. The events of the past are borne in the
hearts and heads of those who lived them. This historical lore is
then transmitted to new staff and leaders in stories, sagas, and legends. The past provides the foundation for the school culture, which
in turn influences much of what happens. The stories recounted in
the culture help members understand what is important and valued.
Much of what is passed on comes through the special language that
a culture uses to communicate its beliefs and values.

HISTORY

It is sometimes easy for us to understand the influence of the past when we look
at generations: the Depression and World War II deeply shaped the generation
of people born in the early 1920s. The war in Vietnam and the civil rights movement molded the baby boom generation. The September 11 attacks and the
financial crisis of the early twenty-first century are key events that have shaped
the new century. No Child Left Behind legislation and the development of state
accountability systems have reframed the notion of school goals and testing. Past
events also deeply shape the culture of organizations.

   The culture of a school is built up over time as people work together, play
together, fight together, cry together, and laugh together. The most profound

aspects of values and relationships come into play as staff members face crises, deal with tragedy, make mistakes, enjoy success, and recognize accomplishments—that is, as problems are solved and conflicts resolved. The end of a leadership team, the death of a student, the life-threatening illness of a staff member, implementation of a new combined math-science curriculum, or selection as a National School of Excellence—all of these events can indelibly affect a school's core norms and values.

The past is truly never far away. People remember events of the past and the feelings they produced. They are also reminded of the past when stories are told. The songwriter Jim Steinman uses the metaphor of an automobile's rearview mirror to recognize the closeness of meaningful past events and relationships. He notes in one of his songs, "Objects in the mirror are closer than they appear." For staff, even ten years is not far off, if an event has struck a chord that resonates in the school's culture.

It is critically important for leaders to know and understand the history of their school. Just as doctors and psychotherapists need to understand the history of a patient, leaders need to know about events that have shaped the psyche of the school.

Why is knowing a school's history so important? Core features of a culture are molded over time through critical incidents, emotional events, and profound accomplishments. Over time, values and folkways are crystallized and buttressed through use and reinforcement. Beliefs about what works and what does not are molded by experience and then hardened by time. Stories carry the genetic code of these values, informing new staff members about "how we do things around here," reinforcing certain forms of behavior, and crystallizing beliefs about collegiality, hard work, and change.

Over time, past events take on mythic proportions and legend becomes reality. Sometimes the past is viewed as positive, hopeful, and energizing; at other times, the past is seen as negative, pessimistic, and discouraging. Every school has successes and missteps or failures. How it deals with the past shapes its present and future. How the past touches feelings, hopes, and dreams is always important to understand.

How Schools Deal with History

Like individuals, schools have varied responses to the past. Some celebrate their history in public festivals. Others have negative histories, and staff members continue to harbor anger about past events. Wounds are left to fester, infecting the present with a pessimistic, negative tone. This negativity spawns widespread fear that problems of the past will repeat themselves in hurtful ways.

Still other schools suffer from historical amnesia. People refuse to acknowledge and honor the past, believing that only the present and the future are important. They are in organizational denial, a dangerous and unproductive state of mind.

A learning organization is one that mines past and present experiences for important lessons and principles. Through trial and error, people learn what works and what does not. Across time, triumphs and tragedy accumulate in cultural codes—a legacy of shared wisdom that lets people know what is the best or right thing to do. Recounting history transmits these important precepts, giving meaning to cultural practices and ways.

Without roots, an organization wanders aimlessly, often repeating past mistakes and failing to learn from success. Consider this example: a Broward County, Florida, principal was describing a past year's disaster. She had been trying to instill in teachers a sense of empowerment, a feeling that they could take charge and make decisions on their own, and so she arranged for a consultant from a local bank to offer a daylong session on empowerment. But in the midst of the session, teachers revolted and asked the consultant to leave. They did not see his message as relevant or of much help. The principal was devastated and vowed never again to try to empower the school's teachers. As her story ended, an observer said, "Wait a minute. Didn't that event demonstrate that teachers could take charge? In trashing the empowerment session, teachers empowered themselves. What a great lesson—as long as it is made explicit. You thought you failed. In fact, you were a resounding success. Why not write the history that way?"

How does the history of your school affect its culture today? As we noted at the beginning of this chapter, the elements and character of organizational culture are initiated at a school's inception, shaped by critical incidents, forged by controversy and conflict, and crystallized by use and reinforcement (Schein, 1985; Deal and Kennedy, 1982; Deal and Peterson, 2009). The culture becomes what it is over time as people cope with problems, establish routines and rituals, and develop traditions and ceremonies that strengthen and sustain the underlying norms, values, and beliefs. Over time, informal ideas crystallize into shared norms and values. Core assumptions become taken-for-granted rules that cannot be broken.

Cultural Assessment

Cultural patterns and traditions evolve over time. What forces nudge a culture in one direction or another? Formal and informal leaders articulate direction and purpose through words and deeds. Crises and controversies forge new values and norms in the ongoing crucible of tension and strife. People, through everyday activities, spin unstated rules governing relationship and conflict. Planned change leaves its own legacy of traces and mementos. Cycles of birth, death, and renewal leave a rich sediment of secrets and sentiment. To lead a school successfully one must know the history of a school's culture.

ACTIVITIES FOR ASSESSING THE HISTORY OF YOUR SCHOOL

Get an Initial Reading of the School

A school leader can get an initial reading of a school by asking a few key questions about its founding, its traditions, and past key events of the school.

Look for positive, living roots of the culture, such as

- A deep sense of purpose that has persisted and become stronger
- Continuing stability in core values
- A sense of joy, connectedness, and trust
- Behaviors and traditions that nurture positive values
- A sense of accomplishment, but also responsiveness to the possibility of improvement
- An honest feeling of confidence that the staff can solve problems
- A level of trust among staff members and between the staff and the administration that generates collegiality

Look also for negative or dead roots that poison the culture, such as

- A fragmented sense of direction
- A collection of negative or damaged values and beliefs

- A shared sense of frustration and fear of change
- Behaviors and actions that damage relationships, destroy trust, and reinforce hostility
- Lack of belief in the possibility of getting better (low sense of efficacy)
- Relationships that are divisive and unfriendly
- A sense of staff entitlement; a "hotel for teachers"

Crucial Questions

How long has this school existed? Over time, has the context changed? For example, have there been changes in the type of students who attend the school, the size of the community, or grade configurations?

_____

_____

_____

_____

_____

_____

Why was this school built, and who were the first inhabitants? Was the school a neighborhood school, a magnet school, or a charter school?

_____

_____

_____

_____

_____

When was this school opened? What was the school's design and architecture meant to convey? What does it convey now?

_____

_____

_____

_____

_____

_____

_____

Who has had a major influence on this school's direction, mission, and purpose? What were the core values of the early leaders?

_____

_____

_____

_____

_____

_____

Look at each decade or even every five years of the school's history. Collect old mission statements and compare them. What was the history of the development of the mission statements (for example, were they created through a top-down process or a collaborative one)? What themes do you notice?

_____

_____

_____

_____

_____

_____

_____

What critical incidents occurred at this school in the past, and how were they resolved, if at all? For example, was there a period of high principal turnover, did new programs come and go during one era, or was there a period when staff changed dramatically? What events occurred that transformed the school?

_____

_____

_____

_____

_____

_____

_____

What were the principals, teachers, and students of this school like in the 1970s? In the 1980s? In the 1990s? 2000s? Chart each decade and detail their characteristics.

_____

_____

_____

_____

_____

_____

_____

_____

_____

_____

Investigate Additional Elements of School History

Additional and more complex elements of a school's history should also be investigated in order to understand its culture. Use the following topics and questions to guide further examination of your school's history. You might wish to divide staff members into small groups and have each group chart each of these questions for a particular decade.

Leadership

Formal and informal leaders help provide direction through a sense of purpose and mission.

Crucial Questions

Who were the formal and informal leaders of your school? What did they stand for?

_____

_____

_____

_____

_____

_____

_____

What new approaches, structures, or ideas did they bring to your school?

_____

_____

_____

_____

_____

_____

If your school is relatively new, who were the founding principal and initial teacher leaders?

_____

_____

_____

_____

_____

_____

Crises and Controversies

Crises, controversies, or conflicts forge the norms and values of a school's culture by hardening assumptions in the crucible of strife.

Crucial Questions

What were the major crises, controversies, or conflicts that staff members at your school have had to face over time? What was the source of the difficulty?

_____

_____

_____

_____

_____

_____

_____

How did staff members at your school resolve their conflicts? Did they hold the anger for years or address the differences directly and honestly? Did part of the staff leave because of the disagreements?

_____

_____

_____

_____

_____

_____

_____

Was some accommodation or compromise reached to rebuild a sense of community? If so, what was it and how was that solution reached? If not, why was it difficult to reach a solution?

_____

_____

_____

_____

_____

_____

_____

Are issues from the past still a source of concern or negative memories at your school? How could you work with staff to address those concerns?

_____

_____

_____

_____

_____

_____

_____

People, Personalities, and Relationships

Personalities of the people who inhabit an epoch in a school's history establish ways of interacting with others. They form unstated rules for relationships and interactions. Norms of trust or distrust, collegiality or individualism are formed over time.

Crucial Questions

Who were the people who made your school what it is? What were they like?

_____

_____

_____

_____

_____

_____

_____

How did those key figures from your school's past treat others in the building?

_____

_____

_____

_____

_____

What kinds of relationships developed over time and became the ways of treating people, staff, students, and parents at your school?

_____

_____

_____

_____

_____

_____

_____

At your school, is there a history of relationships built on trust or distrust, collegiality or individualism? What relationships need to be improved?

_____

_____

_____

_____

_____

_____

_____

Birth, Death, and Renewal

All schools experience cycles of birth, death, and renewal among people, values, and programs. How critical times of change are traversed affects future transitions.

Crucial Questions

At your school, how have new programs or instructional philosophies been initiated, implemented, and, at times, ended?

_____

_____

_____

_____

_____

_____

_____

How has the sadness of losing a staff member or student (through transfer, death, or retirement) been dealt with at your school?

_____

_____

_____

_____

_____

What incidents of renewal have occurred as your school has taken on exciting and successful new programs, people, curricula, instructional approaches, technologies, or plans?

_____

_____

_____

_____

_____

What is your overall sense of how your school has dealt with the challenges involved in transitions? Were the challenges traversed well? Were they ignored? Were they dealt with professionally and well? How were challenges handled? Which ones worked out smoothly? Which ones are still causing tension?

_____

_____

_____

_____

_____

_____

_____

Changes, Modifications, and Adjustments

Change is never easy. The aftermath of positive and negative events lingers in a school's collective memory, sometimes for decades. The ways in which the school dealt with changes in programs or people, modifications of goals or educational philosophies, or adjustments of schedules or methodologies are often remembered and can surface whenever new changes are introduced.

Crucial Questions

What are the changes that invoke strong memories for the staff, students, and community at your school?

_____

_____

_____

_____

_____

_____

_____

What changes in curriculum, instruction, or the use of time and materials have occurred at your school?

_____

_____

_____

_____

_____

_____

How have new technologies been introduced and used? How were these changes initiated? By whom? How well supported were staff during implementation? What worked or bombed?

_____

_____

_____

_____

_____

_____

_____

_____

How have changes in the types of students at your school been greeted?

_____

_____

_____

_____

_____

_____

_____

How have shifts in goals, desired outcomes, testing, or standards been embraced by staff, students, and community at your school?

_____

_____

_____

_____

_____

_____

How Schools Face Their History

Schools have varying responses to the critical incidents that make up their shared history. Often, staff reactions to events in the past parallel people's reactions to death and dying (Kübler-Ross, 1969). Some staff members may feel angry that the past events occurred. Others may be in denial, refusing to acknowledge that anything has happened. Some may experience fear, worrying that past problems may materialize again. More positively, some staff members may cope with changes collaboratively, finding ways to move to a successful and accepting understanding of events.

Crucial Questions

Who at your school might be stuck in an early stage of the grieving process? What loss is that person (or those persons) grieving? Who is still angry (even though it may be years after the incident)?

_____

_____

_____

_____

_____

_____

_____

Who at your school is in denial and may need to relive and gain closure about past events? How would you work to gain closure to past painful memories?

_____

_____

_____

_____

_____

_____

Who at your school has worked though the grieving process and is comfortable in accepting the past and moving on? How can you use this individual (or these individuals) to help others come to terms with the past?

_____

_____

_____

_____

_____

_____

How Schools Learn for the Future

Some educators use history to learn for the future. Those who have dealt with events directly often feel internalized acceptance, power, and control. They know that they have learned from experience and can cope with many things that life throws at them. They have transformed negative experiences into personal centeredness. Successful schools nourish the heritage that has brought them to the present. In doing so, they confirm Clark's observations of the reason that unique colleges succeed. These organizations rely on a saga or historical narrative to unite faculty, students, administrators, staff, and alumni to form a beloved institution (Clark, 1972). That strategy is also possible for elementary and secondary schools to use.

Crucial Questions

What are the principles from your school's past that can guide it in the future?

_____

_____

_____

_____

_____

_____

_____

What special myths or sagas of your school can provide guides for your school's future? How could you use these myths and sagas to reinforce the current culture?

_____

_____

_____

_____

_____

What experiences provide a compass to the future for your school? Explain.

_____

_____

_____

_____

_____

_____

What wisdom can your school gain from past events that were not successful?

_____

_____

_____

_____

_____

_____

_____

Create a Visual History

One of the most important aspects of a school is its history. Often, new staff members do not know about the important people, events, and issues that have shaped their school over time. A useful technique is to have the staff develop a visual representation of their shared history and display it on chart paper.

One approach is to involve the entire staff in creating the visual display. To begin, divide the staff into small groups by the decades in which they joined the school (not when they first became educators, if it was at another school). If a large proportion of the staff were hired in a single decade, divide that group into smaller increments (for example, the first five years of the decade and the last five years). Give each group some chart paper and a marker, and have them brainstorm what happened during those years. Some points of their description could include these:

- Major events in the school and district
- Key formal and informal leaders
- Ideas about curriculum, instruction, assessment, and technology
- Characteristics of students and the community
- Key successes, challenges, or crises
- Architectural or social changes in the school
- New rituals, traditions, or ceremonies
- General quality of social relationships in the school
- People, personalities, and social interactions
- Specific events that shaped staff or student concerns
- Clothing, hairstyles, and music of the decade

Post the completed historical charts chronologically, and have a spokesperson from each group tell the story of each decade or other time period. Have the participants add detail to make the decade come alive. Go through all the decades, and then think about the school's history. Look for clues about the values that have transcended time and helped define your school's culture as it is today. In some schools, this activity is a cathartic experience. In other schools, it provides new staff members with a deeper understanding of senior staff members.

Keep the history. One school printed up its history and made it available to new staff members. Another school captured stories and edited them into a DVD about the school's history for use at fall homecoming and other events. Another school put its history onto the school's Web site, along with photos, interviews, and digitalized movies that communicated its values.

Every organization has a history—a set of events, people, values, and crises that made it what it is. School leaders should make sure that there is a record of what happened within their organization in the past, in order to give the school community a sense of its roots.

STORYTELLING

Stories are powerful ways to communicate important information about a school. Too often, professionals believe that quantitative, concrete descriptions of a school—number of teachers, size of the school, grade levels served, test scores—are the best way to characterize the enterprise. Concrete data are extremely useful for planning and decision making, but stories rich in metaphor and meaning are perhaps a more powerful way to tell people about a school and what it stands for.

Stories are key cultural elements, and they serve many purposes. They can help initiate new staff members into the understanding of a school's culture, provide the laughter or tears needed to get through a difficult situation, or reinforce core values and purposes. Stories are powerful, in part, because people can easily remember and be moved by stories that are vivid, meaningful, and clear. There has been a resurgence in the use of stories in businesses, not-for-profits, and schools because they describe the unique quality of an organization, communicate its brand or values, and re-invigorate employees and customers alike.

Every school has staff members who tell stories, and some have identified storytellers as part of their cultural network. Providing time for storytelling can reinforce history and support mission.

Different schools tell different stories, but there is a set of themes that are important. Each story has a theme that reinforces a different purpose. Stories do not all need to be about heroic efforts; the small stories of relationships and hard work are important to recount as well.

Following are some examples of stories and their messages:

- A story about others helping a new teacher who was struggling with classroom management shows how

  Staff at the school stick together to help each other.

- A story about senior teachers who were using a new data system for student achievement and had an "Aha!" moment reinforces that

  Seasoned staff can learn new ideas in order to help their students.

- A story about a teacher who had a unique personality—a real character, but a good instructor and creative colleague—reminds everyone that

  The world is made of all kinds of people, who each offer different talents.

- A story of the ways a faculty pulled together and helped a staff member and her family by bringing meals, covering classes, and sharing sick days after her diagnosis of cancer was announced reveals that

  Everyone in the school is family, and family help each other during tough times.

- A group of stories about unexpected interests (the football coach writes poetry; the art teacher is a judo expert; the writing teacher is a competitive kayaker) can remind us that

  We shouldn't stereotype people according to their background, job, appearance, or anything else. Everyone has gifts that we might not expect.

- A story of the semester when staff members were arguing about which program to implement to improve learning but kept their relations positive shows that

  Even during difficult times, staff members can maintain trust, respect, and collegiality.

- A story about an elementary school teacher who reached out to students who were struggling with problems at home (and about how those kids are now doing fine in high school) reveals

  The importance of teachers in the lives of children and the consequences of connecting and helping during difficult times.

- A story about a quiet teacher who fine-tuned his teaching semester by semester until he was one of the best teachers in the school calls attention to

  The ways in which small successes and continual innovation can make a difference.

- A story of a group of teachers who contacted their students' parents every August, visited their home, and greeted them in their own language reveals

  The value of respect, relationship, and connection in building ties with parents.

- Stories of fun times together as a staff at picnics, volleyball games, or seasonal gatherings reinforce

  The need to play and have fun in addition to working hard as a staff.

- Stories about the successful ways in which staff members worked together to implement new innovations, programs, or approaches illustrate

  The importance of innovation through collegial efforts.

- Stories about alumni of the school who are succeeding at the next level, stories about former students who are leading productive lives as adults, and stories of graduates who are becoming teachers remind us that

Teachers make a difference in the lives of students.

It is useful for leaders to know cultural stories and to become storytellers themselves as well as to provide opportunities for the school's storytellers to share their sagas and examples.

ACTIVITIES FOR INCORPORATING STORYTELLING IN SCHOOL CULTURE

Develop Better School Stories

All of us can become better storytellers. Here are some suggestions for improving your stories about your school. Learn how to tell a good story, and then identify an important narrative that you want to get across or improve on a piece of lore you already recount.

Incorporating several features of good stories can help improve the lore of any school. Here are some pointers (adapted from Deal and Key, 1998; Kouzes and Posner, 1999; Heath and Heath, 2007; Fog, Budtz, and Yakaboylu, 2005):

- Pick a story that communicates deep values or purpose.
- Paint word pictures with rich, descriptive language.
- Be sincere, and tell it from the heart. Mean what you say.
- Describe the people, the actions, and the situation.
- Communicate your values through the story without preaching or lecturing.
- Be simple, brief, and clear.
- Describe how things worked out and what it means to the school and to you.
- Practice the story, and know what the most important elements are.
- Know your audience and how they will interpret the story's message.

In the space that follows, write several stories about your school that send important messages and that you would like to share with others.

A Story of Our School

Setting:

_____

_____

_____

_____

_____

Action:

_____

_____

_____

_____

_____

_____

_____

_____

People:

_____

_____

_____

_____

_____

Message:

_____

_____

_____

_____

_____

_____

A Story of Our School

Setting:

_____

_____

_____

_____

_____

Action:

_____

_____

_____

_____

_____

_____

_____

_____

People:

_____

_____

_____

_____

_____

Message:

_____

_____

_____

_____

_____

A Story of Our School

Setting:

_____

_____

_____

_____

_____

Action:

_____

_____

_____

_____

_____

_____

_____

People:

_____

_____

_____

_____

Message:

_____

_____

_____

_____

Assess the Purposes of Stories

Positive stories do many things for organizational culture. They can teach people what to do, motivate staff and students by appealing to hearts and minds, and mobilize people to act (Kouzes and Posner, 1999; Fog, Budtz, and Yakaboylu, 2005). Negative stories can have a devastating effect. They can teach the wrong things to do, cause organizational anxiety, depress action, and decrease motivation and will.

Describe the stories that are told in your school to other teachers, to students, to parents, or to community members. Once you have identified several stories, try to determine their impact on staff, students, and the community.

Story 1 told in the school:

_____

_____

_____

_____

_____

_____

_____

_____

_____

Core message:

_____

_____

_____

_____

Impact on staff, students, and community:

_____

_____

_____

_____

_____

_____

Story 2 told in the school:

_____

_____

_____

_____

_____

_____

_____

_____

_____

_____

_____

_____

Core message:

_____

_____

_____

_____

Impact on staff, students, and community:

_____

_____

_____

_____

_____

_____

Story 3 told in the school:

_____

_____

_____

_____

_____

_____

_____

_____

_____

_____

_____

Core message:

_____

_____

_____

_____

Impact on staff, students, and community:

_____

_____

_____

_____

_____

_____

Story 4 told in the school:

_____

_____

_____

_____

_____

_____

_____

_____

_____

_____

_____

_____

Core message:

_____

_____

_____

_____

Impact on staff, students, and community:

_____

_____

_____

_____

_____

Crucial Questions

Which of these stories do you want to reinforce and celebrate? Which stories do you want to replace with more positive ones? How do you want to enhance the stories' impact on the school?

_____

_____

_____

_____

_____

_____

_____

_____

Expand Storytelling Opportunities in Your School

Here are some ways to increase storytelling in a school. Pick one you might want to use.

- Hold a storytelling contest. Provide awards and trophies.

- At the beginning of the year, talk about your school's history through stories. What are the key stories you want to share?

- Make audio recordings of key stories about your school, and make them available in the school library.

- Make a DVD of school stories told by staff and students.

- Identify specific times to tell stories—for example, at faculty meetings, during morning announcements, in the school newsletter, during faculty retreats, before special planning meetings, or at the end of the year.

- Keep school stories in written form to hand out to new parents and staff or post the stories on your school's Web site.

- Record and keep track of your school's key stories in a book, on a DVD, in a videotape library, or on podcasts available on your school's Web site.

- Make your school's stories available to new members of the school community and to visitors from the larger community in a booklet, DVD, or brochure.

- Develop a "best of the best": keep your school's top ten stories identified by staff, students, and community available in various media.

SHARED LANGUAGE

The use of words and language permeates our entire social context. Language is a cornerstone of any culture. In schools, a special professional language and other unique words and phrases bind people together, keep outsiders at bay, and reinforce core values. All strong cultures share a unique language of special terms, acronyms, lingo, slang, argot, inside jokes, or unique names for places, people, or events. Leaders need to understand the language of their school's "tribe" and use that language to reinforce or transform cultural ways.

A prime requirement for symbolic leaders is to know and understand the school's lingo. Some aspects of a school's special language may be clear, decipherable, and obvious; other aspects may have hidden meanings and messages.

ACTIVITIES FOR UNCOVERING THE REAL MEANINGS OF WORDS AND PHRASES

Identify Slogans, Mottoes, and Special Phrases

Many slogans and mottoes are used in schools—for example,

- All children can learn

- We share, we dare, we care
- Every child a promise
- Onward to excellence

What shorthand is used to talk about mission, future, and programs in your school? Which items are part of professional language, and which are part of your school's informal culture? Make a list here.

_____

_____

_____

_____

_____

_____

_____

_____

_____

_____

Make a list of acronyms used in your school (for example, POPS, DARE, SAT, DEAR, ASCD, NAESP, NASSP, NSDC, NCLB). Why are these acronyms used? Do they have positive or negative connotations?

Make a dictionary of these acronyms and their meanings to share with new staff and parents. Be sure to translate the definitions into the original language of parents and make the education terms understandable.

_____

_____

_____

_____

_____

_____

_____

_____

_____

Describe Events with Special Names

Schools often have special labels for traditions or ceremonies for students, staff, and parents. An example is referring to "holding an advance" rather than "holding a retreat." At Ganado Primary School in Ganado, Arizona, staff and students hold many events to build professional community. They have "Once Upon a Time Breakfasts" and "Curriculum Conversations."

_____

List specially named events at your school. How did the name of the event originate? What is its deeper meaning? What names could apply to important events?

_____

_____

_____

_____

_____

_____

_____

_____

_____

_____

_____

List Nicknames for People, Places, or Programs

Language can label parts of a culture that are dysfunctional as well as those that are working well. Some words or phrases are meant in jest; others are just mean. Whether they are uttered in jest or scorn, such labels always communicate interpretations about people or events. Here are some examples:

- Lounge lizards
- Dr. Memo (a new principal who liked to send lots of memos)
- Dr. Ditto (a staff member from the movie *Teachers* who taught only through dittoed handouts)
- The curriculum queens
- The young Turks
- The old fogies
- The mavericks
- The explorers
- The tech titans

_____ _____

What nicknames for people, places, or programs are used at your school? Analyze these terms and names and try to understand why they came to be. Are the names positive or negative? What makes the names special? What do they signify?

_____

_____

_____

_____

_____

_____

_____

_____

_____

_____

_____

_____

Identify Negative Mottoes or Other Pejorative Language

Some schools develop negative or pejorative words for people, programs, or events. These terms can reinforce negativity and a culture's toxic aspects. For example, in one school, the governance team was composed of four staff members who tried to take over all decision making. They became known as the "Gang of Four."

_____

Analyze the negative names that have developed at your school. If your school has negative words or names, how did they come into existence? Why are they still in use? How is the school's culture helped or harmed by these negative messages?

_____

_____

_____

_____

_____

_____

_____

_____

_____

Collect a list of positive language, lingo, names, and mottoes that are commonly used in your school. Have these items artfully written in calligraphy and framed for display in the front hall of your school or on your school's home page.

_____

_____

_____

_____

_____

_____

_____

Develop an informal dictionary of words, acronyms, and lingo that are used in your school. One district had over twenty-five acronyms, not counting program titles, unit descriptions, and building names.

_____

_____

_____

_____

_____

_____

_____

_____

_____

_____

_____

_____

_____

Have students collect "creation stories" that tell how phrases used at your school came into being. Try to understand what was occurring in the school and the larger community when these phrases came into existence. Which are positive and should be reinforced, and which should be ended?

_____

_____

_____

_____

_____

_____

_____

_____

_____

_____

_____

Prepositions and pronouns also convey implicit meanings. "They work for me" is different from "They work with me." "My school is a special place" specifies something quite different from "Our school is a special place." Paying attention to the subtexts of language provides revealing clues that can help you discern cultural patterns and ways. Make notes on what you observe.

_____

_____

_____

_____

_____

_____

_____

Positive, meaningful words and their definitions could be listed in a small dictionary or booklet that is handed out to new staff members so that they can understand what is being said and feel that they are insiders. List some positive words that are used at your school and their definitions here.

_____

_____

_____

_____

_____

_____

_____

_____

_____

_____

FINAL THOUGHTS

History and stories, sagas and legends, words and messages are all key parts of a school's culture. Track all of these elements closely at your school. Understanding them makes possible support of positive ideas and change in regard to negative stories.

People and Relationships
The Informal Network

A ll organizations are made up of people who take on a variety of formal and informal roles. These roles and the relationships that connect them are crucial to the effective achievement of goals, the process of decision making, and the central need for continuous improvement and innovation. While the formal roles (for example, principal, teacher, custodian, coach) are important to understand, it is the informal network of heroes and heroines, gossips, keepers of the dream, navigators, and others who move the school along in a positive direction. In addition, the relationships between and among these formal and informal roles are the lubricant that maintains adequate flow of ideas, information, and social motivation. But sometimes the informal network can be negative and hostile, filled with rumormongers, negaholics, and saboteurs. These negative roles can seriously damage the progress of a school. To keep a school's culture functioning effectively, leaders throughout the school need to work successfully with the informal network to build trust and collaboration.

THE SUPPORTIVE CULTURAL NETWORK: WORKING WITH POSITIVE ROLES

The informal network is a collection of roles that develop in all organizations. Each role has a different function and can occur in a positive or negative modality. Leaders must be able to identify and work with (not just control) these various players in the band. The roles include storytellers and heroines, gossips and navigators, among other roles. It is crucial to support and encourage the positive roles described below in order to ensure a vibrant, communicative culture.

Priests and Priestesses

Priests and priestesses guard cultural values and beliefs. They socialize new members of their school community into cultural folkways and share the school's history on special occasions. Leaders help these individuals to reinforce positive cultural values by providing them a forum to connect with new staff.

Crucial Questions

Who in your school takes on the role of priest or priestess? How did they become the keepers of the values? How do they serve the purposes and values of the school? What is your relationship with people in these roles?

_____

_____

_____

_____

_____

_____

_____

_____

_____

_____

How can you enhance how you work with the priests or priestesses in your school? How can you help them support your school's culture and motivate members of your community in positive ways?

_____

_____

_____

_____

_____

_____

_____

Storytellers

Storytellers are key members of the cultural network. They influence their school's culture by recounting stories of purpose, direction, and caring. Storytellers see the importance of actions, which are then honored in myths, sagas, legends, and stories. Storytellers also provide entertainment and support for positive values and beliefs. But storytellers need an outlet. Provide them time at faculty meetings, digitally record their stories for use at closing ceremonies or retirements, or put podcasts of the stories on the school Web site.

Crucial Questions

Who in your school takes on the role of storyteller? How did they become the storytellers? How do they reinforce the purposes and values of your school's culture? What is your relationship with people in these roles?

_____

_____

_____

_____

_____

_____

_____

_____

_____

_____

_____

How can you enhance how you work with storytellers in your school? How do you help them support your school's culture and motivate members of your community in positive ways?

_____

_____

_____

_____

_____

_____

Gossips

Gossips exist in all organizations because they provide immediate access to information and data that everyone wants to know. Few secrets evade their attention. There are very few organizations, if any, in which secrets are kept safely in airtight vaults. People of both genders play the role of gossip. One must know male and female gossips as they are connected to different networks. For the most part, gossips share whatever information is important. As we shall see later in this chapter, in toxic cultures, the gossips are rumor mongers who pass only negative information. Leaders need to regularly provide gossips with positive stories and messages so they have something to pass on to others. Working with gossips is a key to working effectively with a school's culture.

Crucial Questions

Who in your school takes on the role of gossip? How did they become sources of real-time information? How do they support the purposes and values of your school? What is your relationship with people in these roles?

_____

_____

_____

_____

_____

_____

_____

_____

_____

_____

_____

_____

How can you best use gossips' communication paths?

_____

_____

_____

_____

_____

_____

_____

Spies

Spies secretly watch everything that is happening. Spies are intelligence gatherers for staff. They want to know what administrators are thinking and what department leaders or leaders at each grade level are planning. Spies keep some people informed and others out of the loop. Spies who support the mission of the school want to know what's happening. Let them into secrets of good things about to happen and successes not yet reported.

Crucial Questions

Who in your school takes on the role of spy? How did they become clandestine observers? What are they trying to accomplish? How do they support or undermine the purposes and values of your school? What is your relationship with people in these roles?

_____

_____

_____

_____

_____

_____

_____

_____

_____

_____

_____

_____

How can you enhance how you work with spies? How can you help them support your school's culture and motivate members of your community in positive ways?

_____

_____

_____

_____

_____

_____

_____

Heroines and Heroes

Heroines and heroes are the constant role models and icons for what is good. They support and represent what is best about a school; they are emblems and symbols of the good. They inspire us to be better than we think we can be. Find ways in faculty meetings, on the school's Web site, and in newsletters to commemorate the positive actions of these people—whether present or departed. It is essential to recognize and celebrate these messengers of good.

Crucial Questions

Who in your school takes on the central role of heroine or hero? How did they become heroines or heroes? What is their story? How does their modeling support the purposes and values of the school? What is your relationship with these symbols of the school?

_____

_____

_____

_____

_____

_____

_____

_____

_____

_____

_____

_____

_____

How can you enhance your work with the heroines and heroes at your school? How can you recount their accomplishments humbly as a way of supporting the core values of your school's culture?

_____

_____

_____

_____

_____

_____

_____

_____

_____ ✳ _____

Beyond the generic informal roles that we have just described, schools often develop their own homegrown roles that serve unique needs. These sometimes include the following roles.

Keepers of the Dream

Keepers of the dream remind staff that the school has been through rough times before and has always come through with shining colors. These positive staff members are not Pollyannas; they do, as Collins (2001) says, "confront the brutal facts." But they believe in the possibility of success. Find ways to help these individuals communicate their hopes and dreams.

Crucial Questions

Who takes the role of keeper of the dream in your school? Do different people become keepers of the dream at different times? How do they support the purposes and values of the school? What is your relationship with people in these roles?

_____

_____

_____

_____

_____

_____

_____

_____

_____

_____

_____

How can you enhance how you work with keepers of the dream at your school? How can you provide the necessary stage to support or enhance their actions?

_____

_____

_____

_____

_____

_____

_____

Navigators

Navigators help the ship of state steer clear of the reefs and shoals of a long journey into challenging territory. They can see what obstacles to evade and point to clear pathways, but always reinforce the need to move ahead toward greater success. Put navigators on key committees and in places where they can provide direction.

Crucial Questions

Who in your school takes on the role of navigator? Do different people become navigators at different times? How did they become navigators, and why? How do they support the purposes and values of your school? What is your relationship with people in these roles?

_____

_____

_____

_____

_____

_____

_____

_____

_____

_____

_____

_____

_____

_____

How can you enhance how you work with navigators at your school? How can you provide the necessary equipment and support to enhance their actions? How does their work connect with the core values of the school culture?

_____

_____

_____

_____

_____

_____

_____

_____

_____

Nodes

Nodes are the computer routers of a school's culture, circulating official or timely information throughout the school. They transmit what is happening at their school in regard to instruction; pass around articles on new research, new approaches, or best practices; and know of every workshop that pertains to school goals. Unlike gossips, nodes concentrate on programmatic and technical information rather than social information. Make sure these individuals have information about the school so they can route it to the right people.

Crucial Questions

Who at your school takes on the role of node? How did they become the information routers for your school? How do they support the purposes and goals of the school? What is your relationship with people in these roles?

_____

_____

_____

_____

_____

_____

_____

_____

_____

_____

How can you help the nodes at your school gather more information of importance? How can you help them support your school's culture and motivate members of your community in positive ways?

_____

_____

_____

_____

_____

_____

_____

_____

Compasses

Compasses know where true north lies and help wavering souls stay on course.
Like priests or priestesses, they are grounded in the deep core values of education.

They are spirit guides who help to maintain attention on and movement toward education's most profound purposes. Spend time with those who serve as compasses and put them in situations where they can help reinforce core values.

Crucial Questions

Who in your school takes on the role of compass? How did they become so genuinely connected to the purposes of education? Why are their values so deeply held? How do they support the purposes and values of your school? What is your relationship with people in these roles?

_____

_____

_____

_____

_____

_____

_____

_____

_____

_____

_____

_____

_____

_____

_____

How can you enhance the message of the compasses at your school? How can you help them support your school's culture and motivate members of your community in positive ways?

_____

_____

_____

_____

_____

_____

_____

Explorers and Pioneers

Explorers enjoy the risk and rewards of trying new approaches even when they fail. Explorers are the first to try new things. Pioneers become aware of new technologies or techniques once the explorers have investigated their use. Pioneers put down roots by providing solid, ongoing implementation of the ideas that the explorers have discovered. Both explorers and pioneers are needed for innovation. Ensure that explorers can attend workshops to gather new ideas. Provide support and resources for pioneers who want to implement new techniques.

Crucial Questions

Who in your school takes on the role of explorer? Who in your school takes on the role of pioneer? How did they come to take on these roles? Why are they comfortable in these roles? How do they support the purposes and values of school innovation? What is your relationship with people in these roles?

_____

_____

_____

_____

_____

_____

_____

_____

_____

_____

_____

_____

_____

_____

_____

How can you support both inquiry into innovation by explorers and institutionalization of innovation by pioneers? How can you help them support your school's culture and motivate members of your school's community to try new ideas and approaches?

_____

_____

_____

_____

_____

_____

_____

_____

_____

_____

THE NOXIOUS NETWORK: DEALING WITH TOXIC ROLES

The noxious network is a collection of negative, hostile, or nasty roles that develop in some settings. Each hostile role has a different function and can influence a school in a negative direction. Leaders must be able to identify and cope with these septic roles. The roles include spies and saboteurs, negaholics and vultures, among other roles. Because the people in these roles can destroy trust, commitment, and collaboration, leaders must work to reduce the influence of these toxic individuals.

Destructive Spies

Destructive spies seek out information in order to squash or damage any effort to make things better or to change toxic attitudes into positive efforts. Leaders need to have information to counter these individuals and must lessen their access to others.

Crucial Questions

Who in your school takes on the role of destructive spy? How did they become so negative? How do they damage the purposes and values of your school's culture? What is your relationship with people in these roles?

_____

_____

_____

_____

_____

_____

_____

_____

_____

_____

How can you enhance how you work with destructive spies? How can you lessen their impact, protect the positive aspects of your school's culture, or remove their influence?

_____

_____

_____

_____

_____

_____

_____

Saboteurs

Saboteurs find ways to sabotage, damage, or incapacitate new ideas or programs. They are aware of everyone's weaknesses and use them to their own advantage. Either through small attacks (death by a thousand cuts) or frontal attacks (major artillery), they kill new ideas and initiative. School leaders must be able to defuse these roadside bombs, decrease their informal influence, and be able to demonstrate the potential of new ideas.

Crucial Questions

Who in your school takes on the role of saboteur? How did they become so negative and hostile? How do they damage the purposes and values of your school's culture? What weapons do they use in their attacks? How can you counter those attacks? What is your relationship with people in these roles?

_____

_____

_____

_____

_____

_____

_____

_____

_____

_____

_____

_____

_____

_____

_____

_____

How can you enhance how you work with saboteurs? How can you lessen their impact, protect the positive aspects of your school's culture, or remove their influence?

_____

_____

_____

_____

_____

_____

_____

Pessimistic Tale-Tellers

Pessimistic tale-tellers recount the stories of every failure, unresolved issue, or lost opportunity. They poison a school's culture with negative stories that dampen energy and destroy people's willingness to work together to improve their school. All organizations have things that aren't right or haven't gone right; but they don't necessarily dwell on these stories of woe. Leaders need to provide few forums for these speakers and to have positive examples to counter their negative tales.

Crucial Questions

Who in your school takes on the role of pessimistic tale-teller? How did they become so negative and hostile? What are they trying to accomplish? How do they damage the purposes and values of your school's culture? What is your relationship with people in these roles?

_____

_____

_____

_____

_____

_____

_____

_____

_____

_____

_____

_____

_____

_____

How can you enhance how you work with pessimistic tale-tellers? How do you lessen their impact, protect the positive aspects of your school's culture, or remove their influence?

_____

_____

_____

_____

_____

_____

_____

Keepers of the Nightmare

Keepers of the nightmare remind staff members of dreams that went awry, hopes that were dashed, and past programs that never worked. Unlike keepers of the dream, keepers of the nightmare want things to fail, either for their own benefit or because of some jaded sense of doom. They constantly hark back to prior failures or marginal successes, keeping members of the school community off balance and doubting that they can move forward. All schools have had programs that have not lived up to their hype. Everyone needs to accept the mistakes, but then move on to new programs that can serve students.

Crucial Questions

Who in your school takes on the role of keeper of the nightmare? How did they become so negative and hostile? How do they damage the purposes and values of your school's culture? What is your relationship with people in these roles?

_____

_____

_____

_____

_____

_____

_____

_____

_____ı_____

_____

_____

How can you enhance how you work with keepers of the nightmare? How can you lessen their impact, protect the positive aspects of your school's culture, or remove their influence?

_____

_____

_____

_____

_____

_____

_____

Negaholics

Negaholics are addicted to negativity (Carter-Scott, 1991). They are efficient, constant, and ruthless in finding fault with everything. They damage motivation, conversation, effort, and commitment. These are not honest critics who keep one aware of possible unintended consequences; negaholics want everyone to believe that trying to improve is futile, if not insane. Leaders can reduce the impact of negaholics by allowing honest critiques while ensuring that positive analysis and support for new ideas are heard.

Crucial Questions

Who in your school takes on the role of negaholic? How did they become so negative and hostile? What tactics do they use to attack people and programs? How can you counter these approaches? How do they damage the purposes and values of your school's culture? What is your relationship with people in these roles?

_____

_____

_____

_____

_____

_____

_____

_____

_____

_____

_____

_____

_____

_____

_____

How can you enhance how you work with negaholics? How can you lessen their impact, protect the positive aspects of your school's culture, or remove their influence?

_____

_____

_____

_____

_____

_____

_____

Prima Donnas

Prima donnas want more than their share of recognition, adulation, and attention. They feel entitled and often misunderstood. Of course, they feel that others do not deserve recognition as much as they do and so they try to reduce the celebration of others' contributions, thus damaging their school's culture. Over time, prima donnas pull the spotlight to themselves, and the community of their colleagues suffers. Schools should recognize everyone's contributions in ceremonies and celebrations, thus demonstrating the accomplishments of all rather than one.

Crucial Questions

Who in your school takes the role of prima donna? How did they become so negative and hostile? Why do they want or need the spotlight? How do they damage the purposes and values of your school's culture? What is your relationship with people in these roles?

_____

_____

_____

_____

_____

_____

_____

_____

_____

_____

_____

_____

_____

_____

How can you enhance how you work with prima donnas? How can you lessen their impact, protect the positive aspects of your school's culture, or remove their influence?

_____

_____

_____

_____

_____

_____

_____

Space Cadets

Space cadets have no idea what is going on and will try anything that is new. They are mindless, provide boring input, and generally take up important time with unimportant matters. Schools that model effective collaboration and decision making often lessen the impact of space cadets.

Crucial Questions

Who in your school takes on the role of space cadet? How did they become so spaced out? How do they damage the purposes and values of your school's culture? What is your relationship with people in these roles?

_____

_____

_____

_____

_____

_____

_____

_____

_____

_____

_____

How can you enhance how you work with space cadets? How can you lessen their impact, protect the positive aspects of your school's culture, or remove their influence?

_____

_____

_____

_____

_____

_____

Martyrs

Martyrs think they have made a unique personal sacrifice to work in their school or to engage in staff collaboration. They may have deep personal needs. Martyrs and their issues may draw energy and time away from the real work that needs to be done. Schools should note the hard work of individuals, but not allow individuals to wallow in self-pity.

Crucial Questions

Who in your school takes on the role of martyr? How did they come to believe that they had made such a sacrifice? How do they damage the purposes and values of your school's culture? What is your relationship with people in these roles?

_____

_____

_____

_____

_____

_____

_____

_____

_____

How can you enhance how you work with martyrs and show them that while they are appreciated, their contributions are not unusual or even stellar? How can you lessen their impact, protect the positive aspects of your school's culture, or remove their influence?

_____

_____

_____

_____

_____

_____

_____

Rogue Pirates

Rogue pirates steal ideas, techniques, approaches, and materials from everyone and never give anyone else any credit. They also bury their own ideas so that others won't find them. They hide their own ideas from staff for fear that they will be stolen and applied in other classrooms. Rogue pirates in a school promote a protectionist culture and send collaboration underground. Staff and principals can change a culture of pirating to one of collegiality by always noting who developed ideas, techniques, and new approaches—giving credit where credit is due.

Crucial Questions

Who in your school takes on the role of rogue pirate? Why did they decide to steal the ideas and approaches of others? What is your relationship with people in these roles?

_____

_____

_____

_____

_____

_____

_____

_____

How can you enhance how you work with rogue pirates? How can you lessen their impact, protect the positive aspects of your school's culture, or remove their influence?

_____

_____

_____

_____

_____

_____

_____

Equipment and Resource Vultures

Equipment and resource vultures are ready to snatch up any resource that is available. They are right there to claim new technology or extra resources. When a teacher retires, they are in the teacher's old room the same night to seize anything that isn't nailed down. Their self-interested behavior damages their school community's sense of colleagueship and shared ownership and lessens commitment to the school community on the part of new staff members who have come into their position with few materials, little technology, or inadequate furniture. Schools can avoid the trap of "first come, first served" by establishing a process for allocating scarce resources and ensuring that newly hired staff have adequate equipment.

Crucial Questions

Who in your school takes on the role of equipment and resource vulture? How did they become so self-serving and grasping? How do they damage the purposes and values of your school's culture? What is your relationship with people in these roles?

_____

_____

_____

_____

_____

_____

_____

_____

_____

_____

How can you enhance how you work with equipment and resource vultures? How can you lessen their impact, protect the positive aspects of your school's culture, remove their influence, and protect resources?

_____

_____

_____

_____

_____

_____

_____

_____

_____

Deadwood, Driftwood, and Ballast

Individuals who take the roles of deadwood, driftwood, and ballast are along for the ride, the credit, and the joy of working in a good school. Deadwood staff members, as the name implies, are not growing, changing, and helping out. Driftwood staff members float along on the waves of others' activity, passively allowing the world to shift, but seldom assisting in any way. Staff members who act as ballast weigh down the school during good times and must be dragged along during innovation. These staff members seldom have the energy and innovative spirit to help their school's culture thrive. People in these roles are noted for their passivity, their lack of true commitment, and their creative avoidance of committee service. School leaders need to find ways to energize these passive participants or simply ignore their sedentary noninvolvement.

Crucial Questions

Who in your school takes the role of deadwood? Who takes the role of driftwood? Who takes the role of ballast? How did they become so disengaged and uninvolved? How do they damage the values of your school's culture and provide negative modeling? What is your relationship with people in these roles?

_____

_____

_____

_____

_____

_____

_____

_____

_____

How can you enhance how you work with people who have taken the roles of deadwood, driftwood, and ballast? How can you lessen their impact, protect the positive aspects of your school's culture (especially new staff members), or remove their influence? How can you get them more productively involved with your school's community?

_____

_____

_____

_____

_____

_____

_____

_____

_____

Rumor Mongers

Rumor mongers search for negative stories and hurtful information—whether true or not—with which to wound their school's culture. They make sure that rumors are spread quickly and widely through every medium possible. Over time, these rumors may come to be perceived as facts and may require correction. School leaders can counter rumor mongers with a wealth of positive stories or help staff members learn to ignore these hostile messengers.

Crucial Questions

Who in your school takes on the role of rumor monger? Why do they like to spread nasty and negative rumors? Where do they get their rumors? How do they damage the hopes and dreams of your school's community? What is your relationship with people in these roles?

_____

_____

_____

_____

_____

_____

_____

_____

_____

_____

_____

_____

_____

How can you enhance how you work with rumor mongers? How can you lessen their impact, protect the positive aspects of your school's culture, or remove their influence?

_____

_____

_____

_____

_____

_____

Anti-Heroes and Devils

Anti-heroes and devils are harmful members of a school's culture, working actively to model negative behavior, negative values, and negative beliefs about students, learning, and innovation. Anti-heroes epitomize poor teaching, disconnection from the mission of the school, and slacking at work. New staff members or disgruntled teachers can be sucked into this type of negative role modeling and start to believe that poor teaching, hostility to others, or simple laziness is what they are supposed to do. Devils are blatantly mean people, replacing caring with chiding, criticism, and overt attacks. They may encourage others to become malevolent and critical. Over time, these types of counterproductive actions can become widespread and normal if they are left unchecked. Schools must counteract the impact of these roles with a strong, shared mission, a deep commitment to students and hard work, and a celebration of those whose work and contributions are positive and meaningful.

Crucial Questions

Who in your school takes the role of anti-hero? Who in your school takes the role of devil? How did they become so belligerent and hostile? How do they damage relationships in your school? What is your relationship with people in these roles?

_____

_____

_____

_____

_____

_____

_____

_____

_____

_____

How can you address the negativity of anti-heroes and devils? List actions that you can take to reduce their influence. How can you lessen their impact and protect the positive aspects of your school's culture?

_____

_____

_____

_____

_____

_____

_____

_____

_____

FINAL THOUGHTS

Working with both the positive and the noxious members of your school's informal network is extremely important. These informal players in the culture drama can often make or break a culture, sustain it or send it into a death trajectory. Becoming an effective leader requires working effectively with both positive and negative types of informal networks.

Architecture, Artifacts, and Symbols

The Visual Scene

S taff, students, and parents spend long days and often years in school buildings—teaching, learning, sharing, growing. It is important to realize that the architecture of the building sends a message about what is important and valued. The physical environment in many ways can reinforce or suppress commitment to the school. Within the building the symbols and artifacts of the school's culture become messages of deeper values and purpose. All the characteristics of the visual scene are key aspects leaders use to reinforce the culture.

ARCHITECTURE AND ENVIRONMENT

Where we work and learn has a powerful impact. The architecture and physical environment of a school affect our emotional state and our ability to concentrate, and they communicate beliefs about what is important.

In subtle yet significant ways, architecture and the physical environment play key roles in the culture of a school. Architecture and the physical environment

- Send messages about what is important; for example, is the football stadium state-of-the-art while the library is crumbling?

- Reinforce a sense of community; for example, does exhibited artwork reflect the ethnic and social diversity of the community?

- Communicate core mission and values; for example, are the spaces for learning as large as the spaces for play?

- Motivate hard work and pride; for example, does the school recognize the successes and display the accomplishments of students, staff, and community members?

The physical setting of a school, as part of the culture, influences our psychic state. If we work in a place that is dark and dirty, we are likely to feel emotionally drained, unhappy, and generally depressed. In contrast, in settings that are clean, that are decorated with attention to color and light, and that have students' work displayed prominently, we are likely to feel upbeat, positive, and proud to be part of the school. Certainly, tight budgets make it hard to keep buildings and grounds looking their best, but it is important to remember that beauty and style do not always carry a high price tag and can pay substantial dividends by setting the right tone for a school.

ACTIVITIES FOR EXAMINING THE ARCHITECTURE AND THE PHYSICAL ENVIRONMENT OF YOUR SCHOOL

Every building communicates something through its use of light, space, and layout. In addition, how people adorn the walls with signs, posters, and student work adds patina that affects how people react to the school.

Here are some questions to ask as you walk through a building:

- Is student work displayed in a prominent place?

- Is the school building beautified through the use of art, color, light, and plants?

- Is the hard work of students, staff, and others usefully recognized and celebrated?

- Is the school's core mission reinforced through banners, mottoes, exhibits, and presentations of accomplishments?

- Is the building clean, orderly, and pleasant?

- Do the architectural elements communicate purpose and value?

- What is the school like when students are in class, passing in the hallways, or hanging out after school?

- How do different spaces feel to you—for example, energetic, sociable, threatening?

SYMBOLS

> Symbols represent intangible cultural values and beliefs. They are the outward manifestation of those things we cannot comprehend on a conscious level. They are expressions of shared sentiments and sacred commitment. Symbols infuse an organization with meaning. [Deal and Peterson, 1999, p. 60]

Symbols are representations of deep values and beliefs. They depict or signal core values and build affiliation with others in the school. As expressions of shared sentiments and sacred commitment, they tie people together and reinforce purpose.

Symbols are cultural icons that often represent potent intangibles. The architecture of a school can convey values. A display of artifacts can represent the history of students and staff. Leaders can symbolize vision and values through their words and deeds. They signal what is important by acting and speaking symbolically.

The Power of Symbols

Symbols are key to establishing cultural cohesion and pride. Positive use of symbols can unify a group; negative symbols can fragment an existing culture. Understanding and using the existing symbols of a school can help maintain core values. Ignorance of cultural symbols can quickly destroy a school community's trust in a leader, ruin the credibility of a leader, and damage existing values. It is important for leaders to learn about and understand the core symbols of their school and the artifacts of its past.

In designing buildings, creating displays, writing mottoes, or choosing logos, leaders should be mindful of the signals and messages that are being communicated. Symbols often play a more important role in schools than leaders initially suspect.

Living Logos

Principals and other leaders send powerful symbolic messages as they engage in seemingly mundane daily routines. They are what we call *living logos,* transmitting meaning and values through their words, actions, and nonverbal signals. The daily actions of every formal and informal leader become a placard, poster, or banner of core values and beliefs.

This symbolic signaling is evident in what they wear, the words they choose, the problems they raise, the innovations they suggest, the things they feel deeply about, and what they pay attention to or ignore (Schein, 1985; Deal and Peterson, 2009). Other signals come from the educational books they buy, read, and talk about; the workshops and conferences they attend; the things they notice when visiting a classroom; and the things they write about. All leaders are living logos.

Symbols Across Schools

There are many types of symbols in schools. Following are some examples:

- In an urban school, student papers are simply but elegantly matted with colored construction paper to heighten attractiveness.

- In a western high school, student work of all types—poetry readings, athletic contests, plays, and written work—has been videotaped and is continually on view on a television set in the main office.

- In a Florida middle school, new glass display cases house both athletic and academic awards, with the academic awards at eye level and the athletic trophies below.

- Audubon Elementary in Baton Rouge, Louisiana, has a Hall of Honor where the school has matted and framed newspaper articles mentioning teachers, poems published by students and staff, awards received for excellent teaching, and other accomplishments.

Types of Symbols in Schools

The following examples of symbols cover a range of possibilities.

- Logos
- Mascots

- Displays of student work
- Banners
- Displays of past achievements—athletic, academic, artistic, service
- Emblems of diversity
- Awards, trophies, and plaques
- Halls of honor (athletic, academic, artistic, service)
- Mission statements
- Historical artifacts and collections

ACTIVITIES FOR ASSESSING SYMBOLS AND ARTIFACTS
Evaluate School Symbols

Examine your school's symbols closely. There are many types of symbols and many ways to use them. Consider what they communicate and where they are displayed.

Crucial Questions

What are your school's symbols and artifacts? Where are they displayed and used? What do they mean?

_____

_____

_____

_____

_____

_____

_____

_____

Does your school's display of symbols or artifacts reflect a positive message? If not, how might you change the display?

_____

_____

_____

_____

_____

_____

_____

Assess the Symbolism of Actions and Events

Symbolism is found in artifacts, actions, and events. It is important to understand and consider all the symbols—physical, behavioral, and spiritual.

Following is a list of different types of symbolic actions and events, along with a set of reflective questions.

Crucial Questions

The symbolism of action. What do you spend time doing? What do you avoid?

_____

_____

_____

_____

_____

_____

_____

_____

_____

The symbolism of the school tour. Where do you visit on the tour? What do you focus on when you visit a classroom? What does this communicate?

_____

_____

_____

_____

_____

_____

_____

_____

_____

The symbolism of intellectual engagement. What ideas, readings, and issues do you engage yourself in learning?

_____

_____

_____

_____

_____

_____

_____

The symbolism of writing. What do memos and messages from the principal's office communicate? Are they well formatted, clear, and engaging?

_____

_____

_____

_____

_____

_____

_____

_____

The symbolism of communicating ideas. What educational ideas do you champion?

_____

_____

_____

_____

_____

_____

_____

_____

The symbolism of advocacy. What do you take a stand on? What is important to fight for?

_____

_____

_____

_____

_____

_____

_____

The symbolism of sharing and collegial relationships. What are the times and places for colleagues to gather together to share ideas, a meal, a concern, or a problem? Are these positive times of interaction and supportive relationships?

_____

_____

_____

_____

_____

_____

_____

_____

The symbolism of greetings. How are new and ongoing members of the school community greeted? Are the greetings warm and engaging?

_____

_____

_____

_____

_____

_____

_____

The symbolism of song and music. How are songs and music used in the school? What do the lyrics communicate? Does the music reflect the diversity of the school?

_____

_____

_____

_____

_____

_____

_____

_____

The symbolism of joy, laughter, fun, and humor. How are fun and laughter part of the school day?

_____

_____

_____

_____

_____

_____

The symbolism of storytelling. What stories are told? When are they told?

_____

_____

_____

_____

_____

_____

_____

_____

The symbolism of recognition. How are people recognized for their accomplishments, hard work, and dedication?

_____

_____

_____

_____

_____

_____

_____

The symbolism of professional learning. What is the nature of professional development? Is it a central part of the culture at your school? When and how often does it occur?

_____

_____

_____

_____

_____

_____

_____

_____

_____

ARTIFACTS IN THE SCHOOL: SYMBOLS AND SIGNS WITH MEANING

Every school has a wide spectrum of artifacts located in classrooms, hallways, and meeting places. Artifacts are symbols and signs of school values. Classrooms store symbols of work and learning. Hallways display a mix of student and teacher accomplishments, awards, messages, and mottoes. Meeting places often herald spirit and community through murals and mascots. One example of the conscious use of an artifact is in Joyce Elementary School in Detroit, where an enlarged copy of the school's mission statement is displayed in the front hall where everyone walking in can see it. In some schools, the core values of the school are displayed on pins that staff members and students receive for special accomplishments.

Artifacts that recognize the accomplishments of staff, students, and community members promote effort, focus attention on core values, and shout out that a school has done good or even great things.

Leaders need to help find and display the artifacts of a school and organize them into symbols and signs of purpose and value.

ACTIVITIES FOR ASSESSING THE MEANING OF ARTIFACTS, SYMBOLS, AND SIGNS

Take some time to reflect on the artifacts, symbols, and signs in your school. Assess their meaning to staff, students, and community.

Examine Your School's Mission Statement

Following are some questions to ask concerning your school's mission statement, where is it displayed, and how it is reinforced.

Crucial Questions

What is your school's mission statement?

_____

_____

_____

_____

_____

Is your school's mission statement prominently and engagingly displayed? Where is it on view? Where else could you exhibit it? How could you use technology to make the mission statement more accessible?

_____

_____

_____

_____

_____

Is it regularly refined and continually mentioned by leaders and staff members? When was it last revisited? How do you plan to revitalize the mission statement?

_____

_____

_____

_____

_____

Is the mission statement exhibited in the central meeting place of the school either in its entirety or as a motto or slogan? How could you transform the mission into a shorter and more catchy phrasing?

_____

_____

_____

_____

_____

_____

Consider Displays of Student Work and Accomplishments

Visual displays of student work and other student accomplishments are a central part of a school's culture. These displays, like those of a nation's museums, recognize what people can achieve.

Crucial Questions

At your school, are there display cases containing students' work, trophies, and artifacts from special efforts (footballs, notes from forensics, pom-poms, lab books from the Westinghouse Science winner)? What other artifacts do you want to put on show to reinforce other values?

_____

_____

_____

_____

_____

Does the student work on classroom walls at your school show what routine accomplishments look like? Are these regularly updated with newer accomplishments? How can you encourage staff to make their classroom walls galleries of achievement?

_____

_____

_____

_____

Display Banners, Murals, Wall Hangings, and Posters

Some schools prefer a sterile look; others articulate vision and values through large wall displays. Cloth banners that display words and symbols are powerful ways to reinforce values. Murals can bring together the work of students and others to send key messages about diversity, community service, commitment, or other values. Wall hangings provide an opportunity to brighten up a dull hallway. Posters call attention to plays and movies but are also a way to convey values and recognize success.

At Ganado Primary School in Arizona, Navajo rugs woven in the unique local red design are prominently displayed throughout the school. One particularly large and beautiful rug in the front hall served as the pattern for the architects who designed the floor in the lunchroom.

At Muir Elementary School in Madison, Wisconsin, a large, complex bas-relief mural in the main office depicts major aspects of John Muir's world. The values of the school are embedded and reflected in the mural.

Crucial Questions

What messages are communicated by banners and posters in your school? What is the school signaling and celebrating through large visual displays?

_____

_____

_____

_____

_____

_____

_____

Use Displays That Celebrate Achievements, Triumphs, and Success

Most people want to be part of a winning organization. We feel greater motivation and commitment when we know that we are part of a successful school. One of the key ways to encourage those positive feelings is to display evidence of past accomplishments around the school.

Crucial Questions

Are there displays of both academic and athletic accomplishments at your school? What other accomplishments would you like to display and where?

_____

_____

_____

_____

_____

Do the displays at your school communicate the importance of the accomplishments? How could you make the displays of academics more energized and exciting?

_____

_____

_____

_____

_____

Are the accomplishments that are celebrated in the displays at your school attainable by most people, or are they only incredible achievements that few could attain (for example, Olympic medals, Westinghouse Science awards)? Superachievers should be noted, but the achievement of all needs to be recognized as well. List the types of accomplishments that are not now presented. Decide which to make visible to the school community.

_____

_____

_____

_____

_____

_____

Collect and Examine Artifacts

Collecting and examining school artifacts is both important and fun, but it is often difficult to discern the meaning of artifacts in one's own culture. Following are some ways to collect artifacts and interpret their meaning.

------------------------------ ✳ ------------------------------

Imagine that you are an archeologist who has stumbled on a long-lost ruin that has been hidden in the sands for hundreds or even thousands of years. Walk around the school as though you have just opened up a long-closed building, looking for artifacts and relics that seem as if they were important to the prior inhabitants. Be aware that some artifacts may be communicating significant messages.

Crucial Questions

What strikes your eye as you walk into classrooms?

_____

_____

_____

_____

_____

_____

What do you find in hallways? What is the significance of these items?

_____

_____

_____

_____

_____

_____

What key artifacts, artwork, posters, or other relics do you find in the main office? What messages do they communicate?

_____

_____

_____

_____

_____

Look for large rooms. What do you find in them? How were they used? For example, were they libraries, athletic training rooms, or theater settings?

_____

_____

_____

_____

_____

_____

_____

Whose pictures are displayed? What do you think they represent about the school?

_____

_____

_____

_____

_____

_____

Identify the Most Important Artifacts

Engage the staff of your school in a simulation to see what artifacts they consider important. Ask them to imagine that a fire is sweeping through the school. Luckily, all their teaching materials and records have already been saved, but they need to decide what else is important enough to save.

Crucial Questions

What items should be salvaged for posterity first?

_____

_____

_____

_____

_____

_____

What else would the staff want to be sure to rescue if they could?

_____

_____

_____

_____

_____

Why are these things important to the school?

_____

_____

_____

_____

_____

What artifacts would be important in helping the staff rebuild a history of the school?

_____

_____

_____

_____

_____

_____

What things should be left behind because it would be better to start anew without them?

_____

_____

_____

_____

_____

On a day when the school is empty, walk into the building through the doors that students use. Notice what you see first. What message do you get from the setting? Try to sense what the building is like as you enter it. Is it warm? Threatening? Cold and dark? Cheery and fun?

_____

_____

_____

_____

_____

_____

Conduct an Educational Garage Sale

Determining which aspects of a school's culture to keep and celebrate and which aspects to transform or change is another key to maintaining a strong, professional culture. One way to approach this task is to conduct an "educational garage sale" in which staff members select aspects of the school to store, sell, or trade.

During the sale, staff members will determine what to do with various aspects of the school. Items for the garage sale can include values, programs, equipment, past events, social relationships, curricular ideas, teaching approaches, educational issues, and conflicts. Although all of these are not cultural elements in themselves, each represents sets of norms or values in a school.

Here are some possibilities for the items that can be collected:

- Some items will be placed in a *museum* because they have served the school well and need a place of honor but should no longer be part of the school—for example, an old spelling series.

- Some items are *not for sale* because they are positive features of the school—for example, a successful reading or writing program.

- Some programs are not working well and *need repair*. One example might be a school's behavior policy for students; although it is still somewhat functional, the staff knows it needs to be repaired.

- Some important aspects of a school's culture may have been dropped or stopped and may need to be *reclaimed*. A tradition of welcoming new staff members with a big barbeque and greeting that was dropped one year may be important to reclaim and resuscitate because it is a meaningful tradition that helps new staff members to become comfortable and begin to make connections with their colleagues (Michael Bernhard, Dean Medical Center, personal conversation, June 2008).

- Some items are no longer working and should simply be *thrown in the garbage can*. These are things that do not work well or are of no use in the current school. Examples include old assemblies that no longer motivate students or textbooks that are out-of-date.

- Some items are highly negative and toxic. These must be handled carefully and *deposited in a toxic waste hauler*. Examples include longtime conflicts among staff members, negative expectations held about some students, or hostility that arises in faculty meetings.

Have staff members reflect on aspects of the school that they want to keep, sell, or get rid of. Write the names of the categories on separate sheets of chart paper or draw a simple picture to represent the category (a museum, a garbage can, and the others). Tape the sheets of chart paper, labeled with the categories, on the wall.

Next, have each staff member write the items they want to save, sell, or get rid of on paper. Have staff members tape each of their items to the chart that represents what they want done with it. If you and your staff write the items on multicolored paper, you will end up with a wall of chart paper and rainbow-colored items.

Once everyone has put up all their items, have everyone tour the various categories to see how others feel. Later, type up the lists and find ways to address the items that need to be changed (those in the garbage can or the toxic waste hauler) and those that need to be repaired or reclaimed, as well as ways to celebrate the items that are not for sale, which are part of the school's successes.

List your items for each category:

Museum

Not for Sale

_____

_____

_____

_____

Repair Shop

Repair
Shop
⟹

_____

_____

_____

_____

_____

_____

_____

Reclamation Station

Reclamation
Station
⇩

_____

_____

_____

_____

_____

_____

_____

Garbage Can

_____
_____
_____
_____
_____

Toxic Waste Hauler

_____
_____
_____
_____
_____
_____

FINAL THOUGHTS

Architecture, artifacts, and symbols can convey bright messages of possibility and purpose or represent dark holes of negativity, pulling a school's culture down. Paying attention to these aspects of culture will pay important dividends for everyone in the school community.

PART TWO

Transforming
School Culture

Healing Toxic Cultures
Action Strategies

Toxic cultures, or negative subcultures, can be quite destructive to a school—to its morale, commitment, collaborations, trust, and student learning. To understand the nature of toxic cultures, it is important to understand how they differ from positive ones.

In positive cultures, one finds an underlying set of norms and values, history and stories, hopes and dreams that are productive, encouraging, and optimistic. Positive relationships abound when there is a strong sense of connection to a school's core mission.

POSITIVE CULTURES

Positive cultures have the following characteristics (Deal and Peterson, 2009):

- A mission focused on student and teacher learning

- A rich sense of history and purpose

- Core values of collegiality, performance, and improvement that engender quality, achievement, and learning

- Positive beliefs and assumptions about the potential of students and staff to learn and grow

- A strong professional community that uses knowledge, experience, and research to improve practice through collegiality and trust

- A shared sense of responsibility for student outcomes

- A cultural network that fosters positive communication flows
- Leadership among staff and administrators that blends continuity with improvement
- Rituals and ceremonies that reinforce core cultural values
- Stories that celebrate successes and recognize heroines and heroes
- An overall sense of interpersonal connection, meaningful purpose, and belief in the future
- A physical environment that symbolizes joy and pride
- A widely shared sense of respect and caring for everyone

TOXIC CULTURES

It is not possible to talk about school culture without attending to its negative possibilities. Most schools enjoy positive cultures, but some are gripped by a set of negative norms and values, a dead sense of mission, toxic relationships, and few positive ceremonies and celebrations, if any. These negative cultural patterns are built over time as a staff works together, fights together, and, in many cases, fails together. Even in positive cultures, these challenges can fester and grow into dysfunctional attributes.

Toxic cultures or subcultures dampen enthusiasm, reduce professionalism, and depress organizational effectiveness. Leaders must address these negative elements in order for a school to thrive.

Toxic cultures have the following characteristics (Deal and Peterson, 2009):

- A lack of shared purpose or a splintered mission based on self-interest
- Staff members who find most of their meaning in activities outside work, negativity, or anti-student sentiments
- A view of the past as a story of defeat and failure
- Norms of radical individualism, acceptance of mediocrity, and avoidance of innovation
- Little sense of community; many negative beliefs about colleagues and students
- Few positive traditions or ceremonies that develop a sense of community
- A cultural network of naysayers, saboteurs, rumor mongers, and anti-heroes in which communication is primarily negative

- A dearth of leadership in the principal's office and among staff
- Negative role models who thrive in the school
- Social connections that have become fragmented and openly antagonistic
- Common occurrences of distrust and revenge
- A sense of hopelessness, discouragement, and despair rather than hopes, dreams, and a clear vision

Toxic settings are unpleasant places to work because staff members often have become accustomed to the negativity and have adapted to the toxic environment. In addition, the negativity is reinforced by the cultural network of naysayers and saboteurs. It is sometimes difficult for them to see their own pathology, let alone change it.

THE ORIGIN OF TOXIC CULTURES AND SUBCULTURES

Toxic cultures form in the same way that positive cultures form. Over time, as the staff and leaders face challenges, try to solve problems, and cope with tragedy and difficulty, they build up negative views of their work, their abilities, and their students. In part, negative cultures develop because there is no leadership on the part of administration and staff to help school members overcome adversity, avoid negative rationalizations, and achieve positive closure to conflict. But negative actions by leaders alone can also start a downward spiral of a school's culture.

The drift toward negativity is often a slow, gradual process that even positive people are not aware of. But over time, negative views of work take over and become the shared way of viewing the school. In addition, over time, a culture can start to reinforce its own negativity. As we have noted, "In toxic schools, the elements of culture reinforce negativity. Values and beliefs are negative. The cultural network works in opposition to anything positive. Rituals and traditions are phony, joyless, or counterproductive" (Deal and Peterson, 1999, p. 119).

ACTIVITIES FOR READING, ASSESSING, AND TRANSFORMING NEGATIVE FEATURES OF SCHOOL CULTURE

Working with toxic cultures and subcultures is absolutely crucial to establishing a stronger, more productive school. A number of principals and teachers have pointed out to us that it takes only a few powerful negative people to drag a school down.

Usually, there is at least a small core of optimistic people who want to turn the culture around. The following sections provide ideas and approaches for transforming toxic settings.

Assess Toxic Situations

When leaders encounter negative situations, they need to reflect on some basic questions.

Crucial Questions

How toxic is the workplace? Which of the negative features listed earlier in this chapter are found in your school?

_____

_____

_____

_____

_____

_____

_____

_____

_____

How did this happen? Was there ever a time when the school community worked together in a positive way?

_____

_____

_____

_____

_____

_____

_____

Identify Toxic Subcultures

Most schools are not universally toxic; rather, they have pockets of negativity. There may be a group of people, perhaps associated with a specific grade level or department, who are keepers of the negative. These are not honest or helpful critics who help their school avoid mistakes; rather, they are continually cynical people who use complaints to gain power or attention.

The following activities for reading negative cultural patterns and assessing and transforming negative features can become assessment activities if you simply ask this important question: "Which aspects of our school's culture do we find positive and supportive of our shared mission, and which aspects do we feel are negative and hinder the accomplishment of our mission?"

Look for any groups or subgroups who take a consistently negative perspective on the school or its programs yet seem unwilling to work to improve the aspects they view as not working. Look also for keepers of the nightmare, who remind the staff of everything that has not turned out well; rumor mongers, who share only gloom; hostile storytellers, who pass on dismal history; and anti-heroines and anti-heroes, who are harmful exemplars. Who is in the negative subculture or subcultures? What negative aspects do they focus on?

_____

_____

_____

_____

_____

_____

_____

As a leader, you might want talk to those in the negative subcultures about their pessimistic views in order to try to understand how they developed their views. Ask whether they would serve on a committee to work to ameliorate the situation. If it is a situation that cannot change—for example, state standards, the type of students in the school, or the socioeconomic level of the parents—point out that there is no way to change it and work with those in the negative subgroups to address things they do have control over. List any toxic subcultures and how they formed.

_____

_____

_____

_____

_____

_____

_____

You could also conduct a search for negative groups in order to understand who they are, what they stand for, and why they are so regularly disapproving. Leaders need to know and understand deeply the type of negativity that is at work in their school and how it affects their school's culture. List negative groups and their impact on the culture. Identify several actions to address their influence.

_____

_____

_____

_____

_____

_____

_____

_____

Crucial Questions

Ask yourself the following questions in order to learn about negative subcultures.

Who are the negative members of the informal network at your school—that is, who are the naysayers, saboteurs, rumor mongers, and others? What problems do they cause? (See Chapter Six for a detailed list of negative roles.)

_____

_____

_____

_____

_____

_____

_____

_____

What is the focus of the negativity among the negative subcultures at your school? What do negative members specifically criticize or attack? When does the criticism occur?

_____

_____

_____

_____

_____

_____

_____

What is the possible historical or other source of the negativity at your school? Why are members of negative subcultures so continually critical? For example, were they hurt by a hostile principal? Are their colleagues negative, encouraging this behavior? Have disrespect and distrust become the norm? Have formal and informal leaders allowed negative behavior to flourish without comment?

_____

_____

_____

_____

_____

_____

Brainstorm some ways to work with the negative subgroup to address their concerns. You might want to look back at Chapter Six and revisit some of the strategies you came up with to deal with hostile roles.

_____

_____

_____

_____

_____

_____

_____

_____

Listen to and Transform Toxic Stories

Most schools have stories of plans that did not work out, ideas that floundered, and programs that failed because they were ineffective or lost their funding. Positive cultures learn from these stories about mistakes. Negative cultures use failure stories to reinforce a negative view of the school. Be assured that there will be some truth in any story. The meaning attached to the story and its consequences are the significant aspects.

Schools face many difficult challenges. Most often, these challenges are addressed and staff feel positive about what they have accomplished, problems they have solved, or difficulties they have overcome. Other times, though, a story can be spun negatively, fostering negative thinking, encouraging dispirited work, and decreasing commitment. Here are some examples of negative stories:

- **The Poor Student Achievement Story:** Students have been disengaged and performing poorly because instruction has not met their needs, but staff haven't changed their instructional approaches in years.

  Negative interpretation or message: Kids don't care and can't learn, so we don't have to try to teach them.

- **The Rotating Principals Story:** The district has replaced numerous principals for a variety of reasons. There have been six different principals in seven years, and teachers are feeling abandoned. There is a leadership vacuum.

  Negative interpretation or message: Principals will always leave this school and abandon us. Staff have to do all the work, make decisions for themselves, and ignore anyone who comes in to fill that office. It's everyone for themselves here. We don't work together for the school; we protect our turf.

- **The Hostile Faculty Meeting Story:** Faculty meetings have become places for complaining because there has been no leadership to make the meetings productive. These gatherings have become increasingly hostile and nasty. (In one school, the staff characterized faculty meetings as being "like Sarajevo; there is always someone ready to shoot you down.")

   Negative interpretation or message: Hostility, complaining, and criticizing every new idea is the norm, and that's just the way it is. If I have an idea in a faculty meeting, I am going to keep it to myself.

- **The Lack of Innovation Story:** There has been no systematic school or instructional improvement for years. No one goes to professional development workshops, classes, or conferences. You don't see much new going on in classrooms.

   Negative interpretation or message: Innovation is not important; in fact, it can cause problems. We are happy doing what we've always done. If someone comes in and tries something new, we will attack and criticize them. Inertia is the norm here, and we like that.

- **The Blame the Victim Story:** Students aren't performing well academically, and several senior staff members regularly blame the students or the district for the situation.

   Negative interpretation or message: It's not our fault that students aren't learning. There is nothing we can do; therefore, we don't do anything.

- **The Staff Isolation Story:** For years, staff members have worked in isolation. There is little sharing of materials or support. When someone retires, staff members carry off everything they can from the vacated room until little of use is left for the new teacher. No one says anything about this, so the vulture culture prevails.

   Negative interpretation or message: It's everyone for themselves here. If you don't get the stuff first, someone else will.

There are many more stories that staff recount that can become a drag on a school's positive culture and send it down the tubes.

Negative stories should be understood and addressed directly. Describe the negative stories of your school. For each, identify the message of the story (both its truth and its meaning), and then list two or three ways in which you plan to address the issues raised by the story.

Negative story 1:

_____

_____

_____

_____

_____

_____

_____

_____

Message of the story:

_____

_____

_____

_____

Plan for addressing issues:

_____

_____

_____

_____

_____

_____

_____

_____

Negative story 2:

_____

_____

_____

_____

_____

_____

_____

Message of the story:

_____

_____

_____

_____

Plan for addressing issues:

_____

_____

_____

_____

_____

_____

_____

_____

Negative story 3:

_____

_____

_____

_____

_____

_____

Message of the story:

_____

_____

_____

_____

Plan for addressing issues:

_____

_____

_____

_____

_____

_____

_____

_____

Deal with Specific Toxic Elements

Staff, administrators, and sometimes students in the upper grades all have a responsibility to address toxic cultures. Following are some problems and suggested approaches to solving them. We have also included activities and reflective questions for you to consider.

Toxic Element: A Lack of Shared Purpose

Suggested Action

Identify the core mission and purpose of your school, and find ways to reinforce the sense of purpose.

Activities

Use many of the activities that have already been described in this book. Return to prior chapters and scan the next chapter for specific activities that will help you examine what your school's core mission is and ways to reinforce it. The more the mission is communicated, celebrated, and discussed, the more it will become shared by all. Describe aspects of your school's mission that are shared and aspects that are not shared.

_____

_____

_____

_____

_____

_____

_____

_____

_____

Survey your school's history, and try to understand how your school's shared sense of purpose was lost over time. Discuss your findings with staff, and then move to building a shared sense of purpose. List actions to take to understand the history of the school's mission. How would you share this history with staff?

_____

_____

_____

_____

_____

_____

_____

_____

_____

Toxic Element: Disengaged Staff Members

Suggested Action

Have staff members develop action plans for their personal mission and the school mission.

Activities

Have each staff member develop a personal mission statement, then list specific actions that he or she will take to accomplish the personal mission as well as actions to accomplish the shared mission of the school. In small groups of four or five staff members each, have everyone share their mission and their plan. These plans could be developed at the end of the summer or early in the semester, then put into a self-addressed envelope and sent in January as a reminder of what each staff member has planned to accomplish. Describe how you will foster a shared sense of mission.

_____

_____

_____

_____

_____

_____

_____

Bring back alumni to show staff the importance of their teaching on the lives of others, in order to reinforce the long-term impact of teaching on students, their families, and the community. List what alumni you would invite in.

_____

_____

_____

_____

_____

_____

Toxic Element: Viewing the Past as a Failure

Suggested Action

Openly address the problems of the past, but then focus on current successes, no matter how small, and make clear plans to avoid the errors of the past.

Activities

Break the staff into small groups of four or five people. Have each group list all of your school's past accomplishments on one sheet of paper and all of the mistakes or failures on another. Discuss the accomplishments. List specific actions to take in order to avoid the same mistakes in the future. Develop a plan for implementing those actions, and write it down here.

Note: In schools with a history of failed leadership, poor planning, and disorganization, this activity can be difficult because so many problems are brought up. In this situation, leaders should informally learn about past mistakes and begin to address them in their plans and decisions. Once there is a more positive climate, this type of anthropological dig can be less destructive. Overall, when schools have had many failures, a great deal of healing is needed.

_____

_____

_____

_____

_____

_____

_____

_____

_____

_____

_____

Consider holding a funeral for feelings of hopelessness, defeat, and jaded perceptions. Share and focus on the strengths of the staff. Make concrete plans for change. List what negative feelings should be addressed.

_____

_____

_____

_____

_____

_____

_____

_____

_____

_____

Increase the number of celebrations of small successes at your school. Show the staff how they are improving learning by changing their instruction. Tell stories of success during these celebrations. List what small celebrations you might have this semester.

_____

_____

_____

_____

_____

_____

_____

_____

_____

Toxic Element: Little Sense of Community

Suggested Action

Build a sense of community by celebrating contributions, developing relationships, articulating the shared purposes and values of your school, and establishing respectful, trusting, caring relationships.

Activities

- Increase the number and quality of informal interactions among staff members—for example, by sharing potluck meals, playing games together (staff volleyball or softball), making time to share personal or professional ideas, or scheduling outings together.

- Increase opportunities for staff members to celebrate their own and others' contributions—for example, during faculty meetings, at pep rallies, or in daily communications.

- Develop a list of belief statements about staff, student, and community relationships with a focus on how to reinforce respectful, trusting, caring relationships. List the belief statements on chart paper and have staff members identify behaviors that demonstrate those types of relationships.

- Organize a "sunshine club" that truly provides sunshine to staff members in need. Describe what the group could do to effectively support staff needs.

- Have your staff create a history of your school (described in Chapter Five). This activity can help renew social relations that have been strained or frayed over time. Conducting a school history can stimulate trust and understanding among different staff groups. List a time you might conduct a history.

_____

_____

_____

_____

_____

_____

_____

_____

Toxic Element: Few Positive Traditions or Ceremonies

Suggested Action

Review the traditions and ceremonies that occur over the course of a year, and determine whether they are all positive, celebratory experiences. After completing the yearly analysis of traditions and ceremonies, look for gaps in the year or the existence of negative or dead traditions. Design and implement new ceremonies that celebrate the positive, active parts of your school's culture. Develop new, enriching traditions to build and reinforce a sense of community. Start small, and grow new traditions.

Activity

The easiest traditions to rekindle occur at major school-year transitions—for example, holidays, testing periods, or the end of the school year. At a minimum, there should be well-designed events to help the school community make these transitions. List the most important transitions in the year and how they are handled. Suggest any transitions that need a communal event to bring people together.

_____

_____

_____

_____

_____

_____

_____

_____

_____

Crucial Questions

Do you have numerous traditions and ceremonies that communicate and reinforce your school's core of positive norms, values, and accomplishments? List the most important ceremonies and how they reinforce core values.

_____

_____

_____

_____

_____

_____

Do you need to end some negative traditions or improve some ineffective traditions or ceremonies? List traditions or ceremonies that need to be redesigned or dropped.

_____

_____

_____

_____

_____

_____

_____

What specific ceremonies can you make into powerful community-building experiences that are energizing and motivating? Describe how you would do so.

_____

_____

_____

_____

_____

_____

_____

_____

_____

_____

Toxic Element: Directly Hostile or Negative Staff Behaviors

Suggested Action

Some schools have staff members who are hostile and negative. Provide these staff members direct, nonjudgmental feedback about specific negative behaviors and their effect on your school and its staff. If negative behaviors go unaddressed, they become acceptable. List specific behaviors that are hostile or negative. Suggest ways to address them.

_____

_____

_____

_____

_____

_____

_____

_____

Activity

Identify a member of the staff at your school who takes a negative role. Provide that person with informal feedback and, if necessary, formal feedback about how his or her behavior is affecting your school community. Coach the person on how to change his or her behavior, offer to send him or her to a workshop on collaboration or effective teamwork, or bring in a consultant to work with the person on transforming negative actions into positive ones. List the actions you will take to deal with this person.

_____

_____

_____

_____

_____

_____

_____

_____

Crucial Questions

Who on the staff of your school regularly criticizes everything that is done? (The focus of this question is not on the honest and helpful critics who point out problems in plans or budgets or ideas that should be considered but on community members who make negative remarks without making an effort to be helpful.)

_____

_____

_____

_____

_____

_____

What impact does this person's negative behavior have on others?

_____

_____

_____

_____

_____

_____

_____

What can you say to give this person specific, nonjudgmental feedback about the effect of their behavior?

_____

_____

_____

_____

_____

_____

_____

Activities

- Buffer newly hired staff members from negative members of your school's culture, or they will be socialized into the toxic subculture. Provide new staff members with positive, supportive mentors.

- "Plant new trees" by hiring staff members who support positive values and know how to work collaboratively.

Toxic Element: A Lack of Leadership

Suggested Action

Work to improve your own leadership, and nurture leadership among the staff. Make leadership among colleagues a valued expectation. Distribute leadership throughout your school.

Activities

1. Conduct a self-evaluation, asking yourself whether you are engaging in the roles and actions described in this book. Note areas of accomplishment and areas for improvement.

2. Next, do an informal assessment of staff leadership. Which staff members are seen as leaders? When do they have opportunities to lead? How are they recognized for their leadership?

3. Then ask staff members whom they see as leaders. Discuss the importance of staff leadership during a retreat or faculty meeting. Ask the staff what everyone can do to encourage staff leadership in your school. Take the suggestions, and use the best ones.

4. Finally, develop an action plan for building and supporting staff leadership through empowerment, new decision-making structures, professional development, and recognition of staff leaders. Describe what you will do, month by month.

Write an action plan below.

_____

_____

_____

_____

Toxic Element: Positive Role Models Remain Unrecognized

Suggested Action

There are always some staff members who are dedicated teachers; find them. Support and recognize these staff members, first privately, then through informal stories, and, finally, in staff meetings.

Activities

Identify staff members who have conducted themselves in positive and professional ways. Initially, recognize them privately for their contributions. Share with them in private the stories of their special contributions to the school that you would like to share with the faculty. If they agree to sharing their story and will be safe from staff criticism, tell their stories to the school during faculty meetings, in the school newsletter, on the principal's daily tours, in podcasts, or on the Web site.

List ways in which you can recognize your school's role models.

_____

_____

_____

_____

_____

_____

_____

_____

_____

_____

_____

Toxic Element: Negative Role Models

Suggested Action

Some schools have individuals whose behavior influences others negatively. Their negative behavior becomes the norm. Communicate with the anti-heroes and negative role models in your school about what is unacceptable about their behavior. Recognize and acknowledge the contributions of positive, energizing staff members.

Crucial Questions

Who are the negative role models at your school? Why is their negative behavior respected or valued? How did they become negative role models? Describe how you might address their negative behavior. What would you say to them directly?

_____

_____

_____

_____

_____

_____

_____

_____

_____

_____

_____

_____

Whom can you identify as a positive role model or exemplar of your school's values? Describe how you can acknowledge their contributions.

_____

_____

_____

_____

_____

_____

_____

_____

Toxic Element: A Sense of Hopelessness, Discouragement, and Despair

Suggested Action

Some schools have dead or dying mission statements. Articulate a clear, compelling, and positive sense of purpose for your school. Make the vision a reality by developing plans, taking action, and modeling its importance. Reinforce the vision by communicating it in stories and words and by "walking the talk."

Activities

Hold positive, well-designed ceremonies to recognize positive accomplishments related to your school's vision.

Crucial Questions

Is a clear, compelling, and positive sense of purpose for your school regularly articulated? List two to three ways the deeper purposes of the school are communicated.

_____

_____

_____

_____

_____

_____

_____

_____

What plans and actions are moving your school toward its mission?

_____

_____

_____

_____

_____

_____

_____

How can staff members and administrators reinforce and communicate your school's sense of purpose to everyone?

_____

_____

_____

_____

_____

_____

_____

_____

_____ _____

Understanding and dealing with negative, toxic cultures is a challenge. Following is an overview of major strategies that leaders have used to deal with toxic cultures or subcultures (Deal and Peterson, 2009).

Strategies for Overcoming Negativity

- Confront the negativity head-on; give people a chance to vent their venom in a public forum.

- Shield and support positive cultural elements and staff members.

- Focus energy on the recruitment, selection, and retention of effective, positive staff members.

- Help those who might succeed and thrive better in a different district make the move to a new school.

- Consciously and directly focus on eradicating negative patterns and rebuilding around positive norms and beliefs.

- Develop new stories of success, renewal, and accomplishment.

- End old or dead ceremonies that no longer serve the school, and revive dying, decrepit ones that have useful elements.

- Celebrate the positive and the possible.

FINAL THOUGHTS

Toxic or hostile cultures can damage every aspect of a school, from trust to commitment, from staff collaboration to student learning. Staff and administrative leaders must work together to transform negative cultures into positive learning communities. Without this, a school will never achieve its hopes and dreams.

Eight Symbolic Roles of Leaders

School principals take on many different roles. They are managers, working to keep their school running smoothly by attending to the school's structures and activities, policies and procedures, resources and programs, and rules and standards. They also play a central role in shaping culture by articulating values, communicating a vision, recognizing accomplishments, and sustaining traditions. The most successful principals are "bifocal leaders," shaping culture through their managerial roles and smoothing functioning through their symbolic roles (Deal and Peterson, 1994, 2009).

TECHNICAL ROLES

As managers, principals take on eight major roles:

1. Organizational planners

2. Resource allocators

3. Program coordinators

4. Supervisors of staff and outcomes

5. Disseminators of ideas and information

6. Jurists who adjudicate disagreements and conflicts

7. Gatekeepers at the boundaries of the school

8. Analysts who use systematic approaches to address complex problems

SYMBOLIC ROLES

As leaders, principals take on eight symbolic roles (Deal and Peterson, 1994, 2009):

1. Historians who delve into stories of the past

2. Anthropological detectives who uncover current norms and values

3. Visionaries who articulate deeper purposes

4. Symbols or icons who communicate values through actions and attention

5. Potters who shape culture by attending to rituals, traditions, and ceremonies

6. Poets who use language to articulate core values and purpose

7. Actors who take key roles in social dramas

8. Healers who minister to wounds that occur during loss, conflict, or tragedy

Both managerial and symbolic roles are critical in building successful schools, and both sets of roles can shape a school's culture. Here we will focus primarily on the symbolic roles of principals, roles that shape culture most directly.

It is important for leaders to reflect on the various symbolic roles they play. In the following activities, you will be able to examine the culture-shaping roles you take on. Later in this chapter we will examine how leaders use administrative events to shape culture as bifocal leaders. A more in-depth description of bifocal leadership is found in Deal and Peterson (2009).

REFLECT ON THE ROLES YOU TAKE

Every leader takes on the eight symbolic roles in varying ways and at different times. Reflecting on when and how you take these roles can strengthen your role as a culture shaper. Examine each role, and ask yourself which ones you take on by answering the reflective questions for each role.

Historian: Delves into stories of the past

The leader as historian seeks to understand the social and normative past of the school.

Crucial Questions

How have you developed a detailed and deep account of your school's past? Do you know what educational and social events have shaped your school over the past three decades?

_____

_____

_____

_____

_____

_____

_____

Have you conducted any archeological digs into the past—for example, looked at faculty meeting agendas from an earlier period, examined old mission statements, or looked through the files for hints of prior issues? List and describe important historical artifacts that helped you understand the culture's past.

_____

_____

_____

_____

_____

_____

_____

Do you have a keen sense of the crises, challenges, and meaningful successes that have shaped the culture of your school? What are these events? When did they occur, and how do they still influence your school's culture?

_____

_____

_____

_____

_____

_____

_____

_____

Anthropological Detective: Uncovers current norms and values

The leader as anthropological detective probes for and analyzes the norms, values, and beliefs that define the current culture of a school.

Crucial Questions

What skills have you used to uncover the values of your school? How is your anthropological assessment of your school's culture going?

_____

_____

_____

_____

_____

_____

_____

_____

When do you encourage the storytellers on the staff and in the community to keep you up on what's going on? Are you on the gossip's grapevine? Do you use school tours as much to collect data on your school's culture as to assess student learning? List the most effective ways to learn about the current culture and that will keep you up-to-date.

_____

_____

_____

_____

_____

_____

_____

What regular routines do you use to take the temperature of the culture at your school? Do you use school tours, informal visits to classrooms, chats with students, coffee with community members, or sitting in the lunchroom?

_____

_____

_____

_____

_____

Visionary: Articulates deep purposes

The leader as visionary works with others to define a deeply values-based picture of a school's future.

Crucial Questions

What is your idea of what your school might become? How would you describe your vision? What is your idea of a successful school, and are you there yet?

_____

_____

_____

_____

_____

_____

_____

_____

_____

_____

How have you worked to create an engaging, meaningful vision of your school's future that is widely shared? Have most of the staff (it will never be everyone) bought into the vision? Do they believe that they can achieve it?

_____

_____

_____

_____

_____

_____

In what ways do you use varied oral, written, and nonverbal methods to articulate and reinforce a shared vision for your school? Are the vision and mission described in words, pictures, and stories on your school's Web site? Do you use meetings, ceremonies, and celebrations as opportunities to share a vision of the future?

_____

_____

_____

_____

_____

_____

_____

_____

_____

_____

Formulate Your Vision

Having a vision for his or her school remains one of the most important things a leader can do. Your vision should be clear, compelling, and connected to deep values about education and learning. You need to be able to articulate your vision in a variety of ways. Examine your vision for your school by reflecting on the following questions.

_____ ✳ _____

What is the vision for your school that you and the school's staff members share? Write a detailed description.

_____

_____

_____

_____

_____

_____

_____

_____

_____

What key components of the vision can be communicated quickly and simply? Is there a shorthand that can be used to communicate the core components? If so, what is it? Do you have a motto that captures part of the vision? If so, what is it?

_____

_____

_____

_____

_____

_____

_____

_____

Does the school's mascot or other symbols reinforce and communicate part of the vision for your school? How is this done?

_____

_____

_____

_____

_____

_____

_____

Analyze How the Vision Is Communicated

How do you communicate the vision for your school? It is important not only to have a clear, energizing, and collaboratively developed vision for your school but also to communicate it in a variety of ways.

_____ ✳ _____

In what ways is the vision of your school community made visible? When and where is it evident? Make a list of all the instances.

_____

_____

_____

_____

_____

_____

_____

_____

_____

_____

In which major ceremonies is the vision for your school communicated? How is the vision communicated during the ceremony (for example, by written, verbal, or symbolic means)? Ask staff, students, and parents whether the message came through, and note their responses.

_____

_____

_____

_____

_____

_____

_____

_____

_____

_____

_____

_____

How are your colleagues communicating the vision for your school? Are your assistant principals reinforcing the vision every time they visit a classroom or talk with a recalcitrant student? Are your coaches reinforcing the values and mission of your school in their behaviors and coaching system? Is the core mission of your school reinforced at every awards dinner? Answer these questions below.

_____

_____

_____

_____

_____

_____

_____

_____

_____

How is the public informed of the vision for your school's future? How does your school communicate the vision to all the diverse elements of its community? Are your school's mission statement and vision for the future presented in a language that is understood? Are community leaders brought into the sense of purpose and shared vision?

_____

_____

_____

_____

_____

_____

_____

_____

_____

_____

How is your school's informal network encouraged to communicate the vision for your school's future? Who is part of the grapevine of communication? Is the vision coming through accurately and without major distortion? Are the messages from the toxic grapevine being addressed?

_____

_____

_____

_____

_____

_____

_____

_____

_____

_____

_____

Can staff members also articulate the vision for your school's future? How do you know? How can you help them communicate more clearly, intensely, or broadly? What key words or phrases are part of the vision and have become a regular part of conversation?

_____

_____

_____

_____

_____

_____

_____

_____

_____

_____

What formal media are used to communicate the vision for your school? How is the vision communicated by telephone, newsletters, memos, e-mail, podcasts, Web sites, the public address system, public access television, films of the school, or outdoor displays? Are the messages conveyed through all of these media consistent and engaging?

_____

_____

_____

_____

_____

_____

_____

_____

_____

_____

Symbol: Communicates core values through actions and attention

The leader as symbol affirms values through behavior, attention, and routines.

Crucial Questions

Do you have a set of routines and rituals that clearly communicate your school's values and vision for the future? Which are most effective? List the rituals that reinforce the core mission of your school, build collegiality, and sustain relational trust.

_____

_____

_____

_____

_____

_____

_____

How do you communicate through your words and actions your excitement about your school and its accomplishments? What words do you use? What tone sends the message of excitement and urgency? Ask staff members what they pick up from your words and tone.

_____

_____

_____

_____

_____

_____

_____

_____

_____

What do your actions and emotions communicate symbolically? What do you pay attention to? What do you appreciate? What do you ignore or admonish (Schein, 1985; Deal and Peterson, 2009)? What is the first thing you notice and mention as you walk into a classroom (which is the comment most often remembered)?

_____

_____

_____

_____

_____

_____

_____

_____

_____

What messages do you communicate in your daily actions, classroom visits, and interactions? Calculate the amount of time you spend on different activities and see whether the percentages represent what you consider important.

_____

_____

_____

_____

_____

_____

_____

_____

_____

_____

How is your office decorated? What does your personal space communicate about your values and vision?

_____

_____

_____

_____

_____

_____

_____

_____

_____

Take a photo of your office from the perspective of visitors. What do they see? What books, photos, artwork, or awards will catch their eye? What might they infer from what they see?

_____

_____

_____

_____

_____

_____

_____

_____

Potter: Shapes culture by attending to rituals and traditions

The leader as potter shapes and is shaped by heroes, rituals, traditions, ceremonies, and symbols. The leader as potter encourages the staff to share core values and dreams.

Crucial Questions

Do you use the yearly ritual of recruitment and hiring as a way of communicating values and shaping your school's culture? What are your best techniques for selecting staff members who share the values of your school? How do you socialize them to your school's culture?

_____

_____

_____

_____

_____

_____

_____

_____

_____

_____

Do you make decisions based on the values and mission of your school? List five major decisions and connect them with your school's mission.

_____

_____

_____

_____

_____

_____

_____

_____

_____

_____

How do you celebrate and recognize the accomplishments of staff? Do you encourage the staff's role models? Do you recognize the accomplishments of key staff members on a regular basis? When is this done? How do you remind staff of the contributions of heroes and heroines?

_____

_____

_____

_____

_____

_____

_____

_____

_____

_____

Do you observe ongoing rituals and maintain esprit de corps through ceremony and tradition? When are your best times for doing this?

_____

_____

_____

_____

_____

_____

_____

_____

What are the core symbols of the school and how do you use them in rituals and ceremonies? List when you use the core symbols of the school and suggest new ways you might employ them.

_____

_____

_____

_____

_____

_____

_____

Every positive culture has a set of hopes and dreams for the future. Describe what those dreams are and when you can best communicate them.

_____

_____

_____

_____

_____

_____

_____

Poet: Uses language to articulate core values and purposes

The leader as poet uses language to shape school culture, reinforce the purpose and values of a school, and sustain a positive image.

Crucial Questions

What language (spoken, written, displayed) do you use to reinforce core values? What key words are important to you?

_____

_____

_____

_____

_____

_____

_____

_____

How do you use language to elevate the hopes and dreams of staff and students at your school? What stories, legends, or examples are especially useful for this?

_____

_____

_____

_____

_____

_____

_____

_____

What are the stories you encourage others to tell about the school?

_____

_____

_____

_____

_____

_____

_____

_____

Do you make storytelling a regular part of school life? When are the best times?

_____

_____

_____

_____

_____

_____

_____

Do you nurture the poets on the staff who articulate the community's deepest felt values? Who are the best poets? Do you make sure that their message is available on your school's Web site, in podcasts, or through other media?

_____

_____

_____

_____

_____

_____

_____

_____

_____

Actor: Takes on key roles in social dramas on different stages

The leader as actor improvises in a school's inevitable dramas, comedies, and tragedies.

Crucial Questions

Identify the wide variety of stages on which you do your work. What are the most important "stages" on which you perform? How do you prepare to be on stage? What costumes are used for different roles? What symbols do you use to communicate your values?

_____

_____

_____

_____

_____

_____

_____

_____

_____

_____

_____

_____

What roles do you assume, for example, during morning announcements, faculty meetings, and retirement ceremonies? Are they always serious? When could you be humorous, creative, or emotional in these settings?

_____

_____

_____

_____

_____

_____

_____

_____

_____

Are there special ceremonies you encourage that communicate values through symbol, word, and ritual? How might you amplify staff and students' connection to the deeper purposes of education in these ceremonies? (See the discussion of ceremonies in Chapter Four for more ideas.)

_____

_____

_____

_____

_____

_____

_____

_____

_____

How do you help staff at your school remember that teaching is a calling and not just a job? How can you use quotes about the significance of education in the lives of people and the nation to heighten their resolve?

_____

_____

_____

_____

_____

_____

_____

_____

_____

Healer: Ministers to wounds that occur during loss, conflict, or tragedy

The leader as healer oversees transitions and change in the life of a school and helps to heal the wounds of conflict and loss.

Crucial Questions

Spend some time remembering the challenges that you and your school have faced. Map the challenges over the past ten years (perhaps from before you arrived). What have been the most difficult and challenging events in the life of your school? How did the school community address them? How did the school community get through the emotional trauma of difficulties?

_____

_____

_____

_____

_____

_____

_____

_____

_____

_____

_____

_____

_____

_____

_____

How do you help to heal the wounds that are the inevitable consequence of change, innovation, or curricular transformation? What are some of the ongoing wounds that faculty feel from past losses or difficulties?

_____

_____

_____

_____

_____

_____

_____

_____

_____

_____

When and how have you helped to heal the wounds of past reforms, programs, or leaders that damaged the social fabric and caused hurt? Are there episodes that still seem unresolved? How will you go about healing those past wounds?

_____

_____

_____

_____

_____

_____

_____

_____

_____

Do you encourage ceremonies that recognize key transitional events (both large and small) in the work lives of staff and students? How do you help people through change?

_____

_____

_____

_____

_____

_____

_____

_____

_____

How do you acknowledge the pain or difficulties of those who are trying to improve their work? How do you heal the wound of a teacher who has been let go because of their inability to improve?

_____

_____

_____

_____

_____

_____

_____

_____

_____

_____

How have you helped cope with the sadness and grief as your school community faced tragedy, loss, or the death of a member of the community? How can you make such an event a time of community shaping and relationship building?

_____

_____

_____

_____

_____

_____

_____

_____

_____

_____

ASSESS YOUR CULTURE-BUILDING ROLES

Think of the times when you have assumed each symbolic role. For each role, describe when you have taken on the role and discuss its impact on the school. If you have overlooked some of the roles, ask yourself why and consider whether you should take on some alternative roles.

Historian

When do you seek to understand your school's past?

_____

_____

_____

_____

_____

_____

_____

What two or three things can you do to enhance or energize this role?

_____

_____

_____

_____

_____

_____

_____

_____

What impact do you have in this role?

_____

_____

_____

_____

_____

_____

Anthropological Detective

When do you need to explore the current norms, values, and beliefs of those at your school?

_____

_____

_____

_____

_____

_____

What two or three things can you do to enhance or energize this role?

_____

_____

_____

_____

_____

_____

_____

_____

What impact do you have in this role?

_____

_____

_____

_____

_____

Visionary

When do you try to articulate a vision for your school?

_____

_____

_____

_____

_____

What two or three things can you do to enhance or energize this role?

_____

_____

_____

_____

_____

_____

_____

What impact do you have in this role?

_____

_____

_____

_____

_____

_____

Symbol

When do your demeanor and actions stand out?

_____

_____

_____

_____

_____

What two or three things can you do to enhance or energize this role?

_____

_____

_____

_____

_____

_____

_____

What impact do you have in this role?

_____

_____

_____

_____

_____

_____

Potter

When do you try to shape cultural ways?

_____

_____

_____

_____

_____

_____

What two or three things can you do to enhance or energize this role?

_____

_____

_____

_____

_____

_____

What impact do you have in this role?

_____

_____

_____

_____

_____

_____

Poet

When do you try to articulate core values and beliefs?

_____

_____

_____

_____

_____

_____

_____

What two or three things can you do to enhance or energize this role?

_____

_____

_____

_____

_____

_____

_____

What impact do you have in this role?

_____

_____

_____

_____

_____

_____

_____

Actor

When do you take the stage?

_____

_____

_____

_____

_____

_____

_____

What two or three things can you do to enhance or energize this role?

_____

_____

_____

_____

_____

_____

_____

What impact do you have in this role?

_____

_____

_____

_____

_____

_____

_____

Healer

When do you try to heal old wounds?

_____

_____

_____

_____

_____

What two or three things can you do to enhance or energize this role?

_____

_____

_____

_____

_____

_____

What impact do you have in this role?

_____

_____

_____

_____

_____

_____

_____

USE REGULAR EVENTS TO REINFORCE SCHOOL CULTURE

A number of yearly activities provide an excellent time to reinforce cultural values. Rather than viewing them only as administrative or technical events, use each of them to meaningfully reinforce core values. These are times when you can shape the culture during administrative events—as a bifocal leader.

Crucial Questions

How can *faculty meetings* build community, engender respect, and value professional problem solving?

_____

_____

_____

_____

_____

_____

_____

When you take a *school tour,* do you see people connecting, sharing, and praising each other? What can you do to facilitate more connection?

_____

_____

_____

_____

_____

_____

_____

_____

How can _budgeting and planning_ be used to recognize and reinforce the guiding principles of the school?

_____

_____

_____

_____

_____

_____

_____

_____

How can _recruitment and hiring_ be designed as a careful process for selecting quality people, a first initiation into your school's culture, and a time to brag about your school?

_____

_____

_____

_____

_____

_____

How can *parent conferences* be used for celebration, respectful feedback, and true shared communication?

_____

_____

_____

_____

_____

_____

_____

_____

How can *school assemblies* be organized and planned so that they build ties among staff and students as well as promote pride in your school?

_____

_____

_____

_____

_____

_____

_____

_____

In *end-of-the-year ceremonies*, how can the community and staff of your school come together to celebrate successes, grieve endings, and identify possibilities for the coming year?

_____

_____

_____

_____

_____

_____

_____

_____

_____

CELEBRATE AND IMPROVE YOUR ROLES

No one is perfect in all eight of the symbolic roles. As leaders, each of us has roles that we are comfortable and successful in, and those should be recognized and celebrated. Each of us also has other roles that we want to improve, expand, or refine. We may not be comfortable in those roles, so we might need more practice in order to be better at them.

Reflect on the ways in which you assume the eight symbolic roles. Give yourself credit for the roles you take on effectively. Consider what you might do differently in the areas in which you are less successful.

Which of your roles are you best at? In which roles are you particularly effective?

_____

_____

_____

_____

_____

_____

_____

Which of your roles would you like to improve, expand, or refine?

_____

_____

_____

_____

_____

_____

_____

What are the next steps you will take to enhance your roles?

_____

_____

_____

_____

_____

_____

_____

_____

_____

CREATE AN ACTION PLAN FOR DEVELOPING YOUR CULTURE-SHAPING ROLES

In the following pages, we have provided space for you to develop a set of action plans for your work. You are constantly shaping your school's culture with your words and actions as you lead, and thinking more systematically can help you become more reflective and more effective at shaping the culture. We encourage you to think about how you would like to read, assess, and reinforce or transform your school's culture on a daily, weekly, and yearly basis.

Daily Action Plan

8:00 A.M.

Noon

3:30 P.M.

Weekly Action Plan

Monday

Tuesday

Wednesday

Thursday

Friday

Saturday

Sunday

Yearly Action Plan

August

September

October

November

December

January

February

March

April

May

June

July

FINAL THOUGHTS

School leaders take on important symbolic roles during daily routines and yearly events. These eight roles of symbolic leaders can powerfully reinforce the school's core values, and they can also work to transform toxic aspects of the culture. When leaders take on these roles thoughtfully and authentically they can deepen the culture and nurture its future.

The Road Ahead

School principals have a lot on their minds and even more on their plates. Each day is full of situations that demand immediate attention and land mines that can explode without warning. So where does a principal need to focus attention and take action? Many people believe that the technical aspects of schools—especially instruction—should be at the top of the priority list. This fieldbook offers another avenue. It is the culture of schools that really matters. Culture is where principals need to devote much of their time and attention. Without a well-focused and cohesive set of cultural norms and values, a school is adrift, subject to the turbulent and ever-changing pressures that dictate the next promising direction to take. Without a cultural compass, a school becomes a weather vane, and everyone becomes dizzy and disoriented, not knowing where to head.

This fieldbook suggests three main things that principals need to do: (1) read cultural signs and clues; (2) assess what is working and what is not; and (3) where needed, change things for the better. The first duty casts principals and other school leaders in the role of anthropological detective; the second emphasizes their analytic role; and the third moves them in the direction of potters, poets, or healers.

READING CULTURAL SIGNPOSTS

As we have pointed out, sizing up a culture does not require a degree in anthropology; it is a matter of stepping back and reading between the lines of daily events. All groups of people, over time, evolve a distinctive pattern of what is valued and how people should behave. Behind language, rituals, and folkways is a taken-for-granted set of assumptions that help people make sense of their lives at work. Every school leader should take some time to decipher the symbolic glue that holds a school together. The easiest time to do this is when the principal is new and not yet indoctrinated into existing mores and norms. But it can also be done by any veteran who makes the commitment.

ASSESSING SCHOOL CULTURE

Some lessons that cultures pass from generation to generation serve contemporary needs very well; other lessons have lost their meaning. When cultural patterns have little meaning, people go through the motions without emotion and find little to connect them with others or with the school. The school becomes a sterile environment in which students, staff, and teachers just put in their time and find meaning elsewhere—in gangs, families, or part-time jobs.

Even worse, in some school cultures, beliefs and practices are counterproductive. Although they may have served a purpose in the past, the old ways have become negative and destructive. They may still hold a group together, but the bonds are now toxic rather than productive. Once a principal gets a bead on the culture of a school, he or she can then try to figure out what is working and what is not. Successful practices need reinforcement and celebration; other practices need to be changed.

CHANGING SCHOOL CULTURE

For the past several decades, nationwide efforts have focused on school reform. Most of these efforts have emphasized technical issues, with the intent of making schools more rational—cast more in the image of businesses (or what reformers think businesses are like). The reforms have been robust and costly; the results have been mixed. But the unintended consequences of wave upon wave of change have weakened the cultures of schools. Across the country, too many schools are sterile places in which teachers make apologies for what they do: "I'm just a teacher." Other schools are toxic environments in which people take glee in resisting improvements or sabotaging change. The real challenge for most principals is how to bring about change from the bottom up rather than simply following dictates imposed from the top. But accomplishing that will take a deep view of what change entails.

In today's world, everyone is for change as long as they or those around them do not have to do anything differently. Change is like a trapeze act. You have to let go before you can grab on. If you let go too soon, you'll miss the next bar. If you hold on too long, you'll lose momentum.

We believe that the act of letting go is an essential step in moving on. Applying this concept means that school principals will need to orchestrate wakes, funerals, mourning periods, and commemorative events to help heal cultural wounds caused by successions of change and reform. For most principals, the role of healer was not written into their formal job description. But we believe that it is one of the essential tasks of school leadership. You cannot shape new cultural values and traditions in a school landscape littered with past failures and shattered hopes and dreams. Too often, principals are told they need a vision when their schools are still wedded to an old history that needs to be jettisoned before people can latch on to a better future.

As you move ahead, be sure to reinforce the positive, meaningful elements of your school's culture while you find the energy to heal the wounds of toxic environments. Help return the cultural compass and sense of deep purpose to your school. Find new possibilities for teaching and learning discovered through a powerful collaborative culture where teachers are leaders and leaders are learners. Add spirit and energy to your celebrations while making classrooms places of deep learning and supportive nurturance. We need to make schools places of profound learning and continuous fun, where colleagueship and caring are continuously celebrated.

REFERENCES

Bower, M. (1966). *Will to manage.* New York: McGraw-Hill.

Carter-Scott, C. (1991). *The corporate negaholic.* New York: Villard Books.

Clark, B. (1972). The organizational saga in higher education. *Administrative Science Quarterly, 17,* 178–184.

Collins, J. C. (2001). *Good to great: Why some companies make the leap—and others don't.* New York: HarperBusiness.

Deal, T. E., & Kennedy, A. A. (1982). *Corporate cultures: The rites and rituals of corporate life.* Reading, MA: Addison-Wesley.

Deal, T. E., & Key, M. K. (1998). *Corporate celebration: Play, purpose, and profit at work.* San Francisco: Berrett-Koehler.

Deal, T. E., & Peterson, K. D. (1994). *The leadership paradox: Balancing logic and artistry in schools.* San Francisco: Jossey-Bass.

Deal, T. E., & Peterson, K. D. (1999). *Shaping school culture: The heart of leadership.* San Francisco: Jossey-Bass.

Deal, T. E., & Peterson, K. D. (2009). *Shaping school culture: Pitfalls, paradoxes, and promises* (2nd ed.). San Francisco: Jossey-Bass.

Fog, K., Budtz, C., & Yakaboylu, B. (2005). *Storytelling: Branding in practice.* Berlin: Springer.

Gordon, W.J.J. (1961). *Synectics, the development of creative capacity.* New York: Harper.

Heath, C., & Heath, D. (2007). *Made to stick: Why some ideas survive and others die.* New York: Random House.

Kouzes, J. M., & Posner, B. Z. (1999). *The leadership challenge planner: An action guide to achieving your personal best.* San Francisco: Pfeiffer.

Kübler-Ross, E. (1969). *On death and dying.* New York: Macmillan.

Ott, J. S. (1989). *The organizational perspective.* Pacific Grove, Calif.: Brooks/Cole.

Schein, E. H. (1985). *Organizational culture and leadership* (1st ed.). San Francisco: Jossey-Bass.

Schein, E. H. (2004). *Organizational culture and leadership* (3rd ed.). San Francisco: Jossey-Bass.

Waller, W. (1932). *The sociology of teaching.* New York: Wiley.

INDEX

Toxic cultures/subcultures, 177–206; activities for assessing, 179–185; activities for transforming, 185–206; characteristics of, 178–179; cultural network in, 9, 129–148; negative language in, 109–110; origin of, 179

Traditions: assessing, 53–54; defined, 41; examples of, 41–42; lack of positive, 196–198; special names of, 107–108. *See also* Ceremonies

Transition rituals, 46–48

V

Values: activities enacting, 22–23; defined, 14; events reinforcing, 243–246; keepers of, 116–117; shields representing, 30–32; songs for reinforcing, 27; of staff members, 10

Vandiver, F., 42

Vision: communication of, 215–219; defined, 13; formulation of, 213–215

Visionaries, principals as, 211–219, 236–237

Vultures, equipment and resource, 142–143

W

Waller, W., 8

Y

Yakaboylu, B., 95, 99

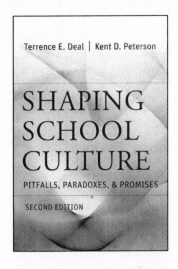

SHAPING SCHOOL CULTURE

Pitfalls, Paradoxes, & Promises

Second Edition

Terrence E. Deal | Kent D. Peterson

ISBN: 978-0-7879-9679-6
Paperback

An essential complement to the
Shaping School Culture Fieldbook, Second Edition

"For those seeking enduring change that is measured in generations rather than months, and to create a legacy rather than a headline, then Shaping School Culture *is your guide."* —Dr. Douglas B. Reeves, founder, The Leadership and Learning Center, Englewood, CO

"Deal and Peterson combine exquisite language, vibrant stories, and sage advice to support school leaders in embracing the paradoxical nature of their work. A 'must-read' for all school leaders." —Pam Robbins, educational consultant and author

In this thoroughly revised and updated edition of their classic book, *Shaping School Culture*, Terrence Deal and Kent Peterson address the latest thinking on organizational culture and change and offer new ideas and strategies on how stories, rituals, traditions, and other cultural practices can be used to create positive, caring, and purposeful schools.

This new edition gives expanded attention to the important symbolic roles of school leaders, including practical suggestions on how leaders can balance cultural goals and values against accountability demands, and features new and powerful case examples throughout. Most important, the authors show how school leaders can transform negative and toxic cultures so that trust, commitment, and a sense of unity can prevail.

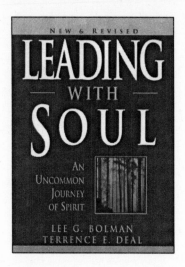

LEADING WITH SOUL
An Uncommon Journey of Spirit

New & Revised

Lee G. Bolman | Terrence E. Deal

ISBN: 978-0-7879-5547-2
Hardcover

"Bolman and Deal understand that organizations are filled with living, breathing, feeling human beings, people who need more than a paycheck, more than a performance review, more than a promotion. This is a deceptively powerful realization for any leader."
—Patrick Lencioni, author, *The Five Temptations of a CEO: Obsessions of an Extraordinary Executive*

"No two authors are better equipped than Bolman and Deal to address and answer the seminal dilemma of our time—the difference between making a living and making a life. They lead the way to discover how to lead a spirited life." —Warren Bennis, distinguished professor of business administration, University of Southern California; author, *Managing the Dream*

Since its original publication in 1995, *Leading with Soul* has inspired thousands of readers. Far ahead of its time, the book bravely revealed the path to leadership to be a very personal journey requiring knowledge of the self and a servant-leader mentality.

Now, in this revised edition, authors Bolman and Deal address such issues as the changing nature of work, the new face of today's workforce, and the greater need for an infusion of soul in the workplace. They also include real-life stories from readers of the first edition, and answer key questions that those readers raise. As vital as ever, this revisited narrative of an executive and his quest for deeper meaning continues to point the way to a more fulfilling work experience.

REFRAMING ORGANIZATIONS

Artistry, Choice, and Leadership

Fourth Edition

Lee G. Bolman | Terrence E. Deal

ISBN: 978-0-7879-8798-5 Hardcover
ISBN: 978-0-7879-8799-2 Paperback

The Classic Leadership Resource Now In Its Fourth Edition!

First published in 1984, Lee Bolman and Terrence Deal's best-selling book has become a classic in the field. Its four-frame model examines organizations in terms of factories, families, jungles, and theaters or temples:

- The Structural Frame: how to organize and structure groups and teams to get results

- The Human Resource Frame: how to tailor organizations to satisfy human needs, improve human resource management, and build positive interpersonal and group dynamics

- The Political Frame: how to cope with power and conflict, build coalitions, hone political skills, and deal with internal and external politics

- The Symbolic Frame: how to shape a culture that gives purpose and meaning to work, stage organizational drama for internal and external audiences, and build team spirit through ritual, ceremony, and story

This new edition contains a wealth of new examples from both the private and the nonprofit sectors. In addition, the book offers updated content and expanded discussions of self-managing teams, dramaturgical and institutional theory, change theory, the "blink" process, "black swans," and gay rights. An Instructor's Guide is available online.

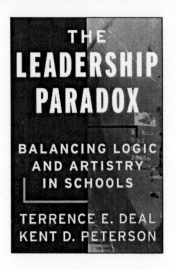

THE LEADERSHIP PARADOX

Balancing Logic and Artistry in Schools

Terrence E. Deal | Kent D. Peterson

ISBN: 978-0-7879-5541-0
Paperback

"School leaders, as well as aspiring principals and observers of the principalship, will delight in this distinctive, playful, and insightful look at the art and craft of leading a modern-day school."—Roland S. Barth, educator and author of *Improving Schools from Within*

"The Leadership Paradox *pushes our understanding of the complexity of the principal's work to new levels. It should be required reading for those who are or aspire to be principals and for those who prepare, train, or supervise them."*—Laraine Roberts, director of research and development, California School Leadership Academy

As leaders and managers, principals must continually blend the symbolic and technical aspects of their role, embracing each complexity with confidence, enthusiasm, and skill. *The Leadership Paradox* draws from organizational and management theory to reveal the art and logic of school leadership.

Instead of viewing leadership and management as opposing factions, the authors show how these two ideals can serve as complements in building a powerful school culture. They also share real-life stories and examples of school leaders who have learned to adopt a bifocal approach and integrate the contradictions of their work.

Practical yet inspiring, this volume presents a wealth of insights for principals, superintendents, school board members, and other educational leaders.

MORE RESOURCES FROM THE AUTHORS

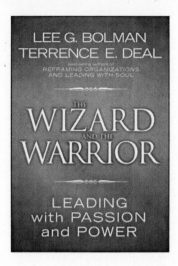

THE WIZARD AND THE WARRIOR
Leading with Passion and Power

Lee G. Bolman | Terrence E. Deal

ISBN: 978-0-7879-7413-8
Hardcover

"The 'gold standard' for looking at leadership. The Wizard and the Warrior is about fighting the good fight, but not losing sight of the magic—it is about making the word flesh. This is a must-read for anyone who cares about becoming a better leader."
—Paul D. Houston, executive director, American Association of School Administrators

The Wizard and the Warrior gives leaders the insight and courage they need to take risks on behalf of values they cherish and the people they guide. Great leaders must act both as wizards, calling on imagination, creativity, meaning, and magic, and as warriors, mobilizing strength, courage, and willingness to fight as necessary to fulfill their missions.

Best-selling authors Lee Bolman and Terrence Deal present the defining moments and experiences of exemplary leaders such as David Neeleman (CEO of JetBlue), Mary Kay Ash, Warren Buffet, Anne Mulcahy, Thomas Keller (head chef of French Laundry), and Abraham Lincoln—all of whom have wrestled with their own inner warrior and wizard.

These engaging, realistic case studies are followed by commentaries that will raise questions and suggest possibilities without rushing to resolution or simple answers.

Armed with this book's expanded repertoire of possibilities, the reader can become more versatile and imbue work and life with power and passion.

CPSIA information can be obtained at www.ICGtesting.com
Printed in the USA
BVOW02n2023280914

368199BV00003BB/4/P